AF204962

The Bigger Picture:

Voices of Africa – Nigeria

Alles Digitale zu diesem Buch kann auf der Lernplattform
allango von Ernst Klett Sprachen abgerufen werden. So geht's:

QR-Code scannen
oder **www.allango.net**
aufrufen

Buchtitel oder ISBN in
der Suche eingeben und
auf das Buchcover klicken

Zum Inhalt navigieren,
direkt abrufen
oder speichern

Dieses Symbol bedeutet, dass zu einem Buch-Abschnitt
ein digitaler Inhalt verfügbar ist.

Various authors

Voices of Africa – Nigeria

Herausgegeben
von Dirk Beyer

Ernst Klett Sprachen
Stuttgart

Bildquellenverzeichnis:
Cover Getty Images (peeterv), München; **Cover** mauritius images / Adrian arbib / Alamy; **Cover** 123RF.com (rawpixel), Nidderau; **Cover** Getty Images (orighomisan), München; **Cover** Getty Images (FG Trade), München; **Cover** Getty Images (passionng), München; **Cover** Getty Images (Vitalij Sova), München; **Cover** Getty Images (Caroline Views / EyeEm), München; **13** Shutterstock (netsign33), New York; **14** Shutterstock (au_uhoo), New York; **16-26** LAGOS by TAYO Fatunla - www.tayofatunla.com/ tfatunla@hotmail.com; **48** © Lemi Ghariokwu; **50** © Lemi Ghariokwu; **52** © Lemi Ghariokwu; **54** © Lemi Ghariokwu; **56** © Lemi Ghariokwu; **58** © Lemi Ghariokwu; **75** Shutterstock (Jaroslav Moravcik), New York; **76** mauritius images / Adrian arbib / Alamy; **125** Shutterstock (John Wollwerth), New York; **126** Shutterstock (Riccardo Mayer), New York

1. Auflage   1 $^{10\ 9\ 8\ 7\ 6}$ | 2029 28 27 26 25

Herausgeber: Dirk Beyer
Redaktion: Astrid Proctor
Layoutkonzeption: Greta Gröttrup
Gestaltung und Satz: Joachim Schrimm, bostext, Friolzheim
Umschlaggestaltung: Maja Merz
Druck und Bindung: Elanders Waiblingen GmbH, Waiblingen

Printed in Germany
ISBN 978-3-12-580014-4

Contents

The Bigger Picture

The Bigger Picture is a series of books and further materials in English which deals with a selection of important topical, social, literary and political issues of modern life, which will help you to form a bigger picture of the world we live in.

Each theme-based collection consists firstly of a series of challenging and motivating shorter texts, in various formats – compact short stories, extracts from popular novels or longer, in-depth feature articles taken from major national newspapers.

Each Student's Book has its own tailor-made Teacher's Guide, full of further ideas and tasks.

To make the scope of the series as broad and interesting as possible, we have moulded together carefully selected material in a multimedia approach consisting of:

- **the texts in the Student's book**
- **short, introductory, warm-up tasks for each Section**
- **relevant sound files**
- **motivating video and**
- **extensive internet links to further reading**

to help *you* form *your* "Bigger Picture".

Learning about the world and its issues should be a pleasure, as well as a challenge. Plus, of course, being able to understand these things by reading and listening, as well as actively talking and writing about them in English, will significantly help your *Abitur*.

Digital resources

The contents of this book refer, in various places, to additional material – links to further articles of interest, podcasts, readings by some of the authors included in this book, interesting websites and Spotify playlists. This is always indicated in the text.

The very first page of this book explains how to access these materials.

Voices of Africa – Nigeria

"Giant of Africa", "pulsating powerhouse", "the face of modern Africa", "a country bursting with opportunities" and not least "a deeply divided country of extremes". Google "Nigeria" and these are likely to be some of the descriptions you'll come across. Dig a little deeper and you will find that it certainly lives up to all of these names.

Since Nigeria gained its independence from Great Britain in 1960, it has matured into a country of many contrasts. It has a huge population: the latest UN estimate puts Nigeria's population at around 200 million people. The population is also one of the fastest growing in the world and experts believe that by 2050 it will be approaching 400 million, making it the third largest country in the world behind China and India. It is a young nation with approximately half the population under the age of 18. It is multi-ethnic and culturally diverse and although English is the official language, over 500 other languages are spoken by various ethnic groups.

Nigeria is Africa's largest economy. As a nation rich in natural resources its economic growth has always been strongly dependent on the export of oil and gas. More recently, however, new industries are contributing to the economy – IT and tech industries are burgeoning and more and more innovative start-ups are emerging.

It is only natural that a country as ethnically and culturally diverse as Nigeria should have a vibrant and exploding arts scene. World-class, award-winning writers, the second largest film industry in the world, a buzzing music scene and up-and-coming fashion designers – Nigeria is truly experiencing a creative Golden Age with new talents appearing all the time who are attracting attention not only inside Nigeria but globally.

Of course, much of what is reported about Nigeria internationally concerns the challenges and problems facing the country – of which there are many. Inequality, high rates of poverty, unemployment, overcrowded cities, pollution, a lack of basic infrastructure, misgovernment and corruption, internal conflict and terrorism.

This book is a collection of texts from very different sources. Some are newspaper articles, others essays, short stories, poems and excerpts from novels, a memoir as well as a play. They have been divided into three sections, which, though the themes may sometimes overlap, shine a light on different, equally important aspects of Nigeria.

In the first section "Nigeria: An introduction through its artists" the spotlight falls on Nigeria's creative talent and how it has influenced and is continuing to influence the nation's identity and its reputation on the wider international stage.

The texts in the second section "The bloody road to democracy" highlight some of the struggles Nigeria has faced on its journey to democracy. They are written mostly by contemporary witnesses to some of the most troubled chapters in the nation's recent history.

While Nigeria may now be a multi-party, representative democracy with a democratically elected head of state, it still faces a number of societal issues, including misgovernance and corruption, internal security issues and sweeping inequality. These are the focus of the final section "Challenges in modern Nigeria".

We hope that you enjoy getting "the bigger picture", and will feel inspired by the variety of different approaches to engage with this truly complex, diverse and fascinating country on a whole new level.

Abbreviations used in this book

abbr	abbreviation
archaic	archaic (no longer in everyday use)
dial	dialect
form	formal
hum	humorous
inf	informal
jdn	jemanden
NEnglish	Nigerian English
NPidgin	Nigerian Pidgin*
pl	plural
pol	politics
sb	somebody
sl	slang
sth	something

* Pidgin is a grammatically simplified language form that develops between people who do not share a common language. Some of the elements are taken from local languages, in Nigeria's case e.g. Yoruba, Igbo etc. Nigerian Pidgin is also called Naijá.

1 Nigeria: An Introduction through its artists

Introduction

News from Nigeria often concentrates on corruption in politics, attacks and abductions carried out by the terrorist group Boko Haram and unrest in the oil-producing Delta region – but over the last few decades Africa's most populous nation has also become a hotbed for the arts. While tribal culture remains an important part of Nigerian life, the contemporary cultural scene has well and truly exploded. From the pioneers of Afrobeat to Nobel laureates, Nigeria is producing outstanding writers, artists and musicians of international acclaim who are helping the nation redefine its complicated identity and come to terms both with its chequered past and the challenges of today.

The texts and digital extras in this section provide a brief introduction to a cross-section of Nigeria's rich and colourful culture. Take a walk through Lagos, past and present, in the company of one of Nigeria's foremost cartoonists, hear from one of Nigeria's master storytellers, gain an insight into one of Africa's bestloved musicians from the man who designed most of his album covers and settle down for a peek at the phenomenon that is Nollywood.

On Spotify you'll find two playlists specially compiled for this book: one that introduces you to some of Nigeria's most successful contemporary musicians and another with the Fela Kuti songs mentioned in Text 3. The links to both playlists can be found online.

Tasks

1. Consider how the arts contribute to a nation's identity. How are ideas about national identity portrayed through art and literature? What does a vibrant cultural scene say about the state of a nation?

2. The writer Chris Abani says in his TED Talk "if you want to know about Africa, read African literature". Consider what you have already read or heard about Nigeria. Have you had any contact—through social media, television or cinema, music streaming services, books etc.— with aspects of Nigerian culture, its music, literature or art? How has this shaped your views and impressions of the country so far? Discuss your ideas in smaller groups.

Made in Nigeria

Text 1: No place does me like Lagos

by Tayo Fatunla (2019)

Tayo Fatunla is a British-Nigerian comic artist. Educated at the prestigious art school "The Kubert School" in Dover, New Jersey, Fatunla's cartoons have been published in newspapers, school books, websites and magazines around the world.

As a former resident of Nigeria's biggest city, his collection "No place does me like Lagos" illustrates this vibrant, pulsating megacity from a variety of perspectives, from its humble beginnings as a fishing community to its status today as Nigeria's economic powerhouse.

ENDURING LAGOS

....RESILIENT CITY

LAGOS – A CITY OF HISTORY AND OF FIRSTS... EVERY MAN, EVERY WOMAN, EVERY CHILD MAKE LAGOS TICK.

LAGOS (EKO) IT STARTED AS A FISHING ECONOMY, BUILT ON A LAGOON....

THE LAGOON REMAINS, BUT WHAT A CHANGE!

IN 1901 **CARTER BRIDGE** WAS THE FIRST TO LINK LAGOS ISLAND TO THE MAINLAND. TWO MORE BRIDGES WOULD FOLLOW. **LAGOS** WAS ON ITS WAY.

MODERN GROWTH HAS EVEN MADE **BADAGRY**, A FORMER COASTAL SLAVERY PORT, PART OF THE THRIVING MEGACITY. IT IS WHERE THE FIRST MULTI-STOREY BUILDING ANYWHERE IN NIGERIA WAS BUILT, AND, CRUCIALLY, THE FIRST PRIMARY SCHOOL.

17

THE **BIAFRA WAR** (1967-70) BROUGHT CONFLICT AND HORROR TO NIGERIA – AND **LAGOS**. AIR RAID SIRENS ... DIVING FOR COVER ... BUT THE CITY SURVIVED!

WHEN I WAS GROWING UP IN **SURULERE,** PART OF MAINLAND LAGOS, THE YORUBA CATCHPHRASE "**EKO ONI BAJE**" OR "**LAGOS CANNOT BE DESTROYED**" WAS ON EVERYONE'S LIPS.

WE HAD CELEBRATIONS TOO, LIKE THE **EYO** MASQUERADE FESTIVAL – A UNIQUE **LAGOS ISLAND** EVENT. IT IS A SIGHT TO BEHOLD ... BUT WHEN I WAS LITTLE I WOULD HIDE AWAY FROM THE PROCESSION IN MY GRANDMA'S HOUSE IN **IGBOSERE** - EVEN THOUGH MY COUSINS WERE THE ONES DRESSED UP!

A SYMBOL OF RESILIENCE... **FELA KUTI'S** GLOBAL **AFROBEAT** MUSIC STEMMED FROM LAGOS, THE VOICE OF THE MASSES AGAINST NIGERIAN MILITARY GOVERNMENTS...

MY SCHOOL BUS DROVE PAST HIS **KALAKUTA REPUBLIC** HOME EVERYDAY. HIS SON **FEMI KUTI** AND I WERE AT SCHOOL TOGETHER...

BUT FELA'S MUSIC WAS NOT THE ONLY CULTURE TO BLOSSOM IN LAGOS. IN 1977 LAGOS PULLED OUT ALL THE STOPS FOR THE INTERNATIONAL FESTIVAL OF ARTS AND CULTURE (**FESTAC**) - THE LARGEST PAN - AFRICAN GATHERING IN THE WORLD. IT CREATED OUR NATIONAL COUNCIL OF ARTS AND CULTURE AND **NATIONAL THEATRE.**

THEY ARE NOW BEING PHASED OUT, BUT **DANFO**, THE DISTINCTIVE PASSENGER VEHICLES WITH FEARLESS DRIVERS AND THEIR AGILE ASSISTANTS HAVE BEEN AN INTEGRAL PART OF **LAGOS TRANSPORT** FOR DECADES.

YABA! YABA! YABA!

...YOU HAD TO THANK YOUR LUCKY STARS TO ARRIVE ALIVE....I DID OVER AND OVER AGAIN.

21

THE CITY HAS GROWN TALL WITH LANDMARK ARCHITECTURE AND CULTURAL STRUCTURES. WHEN IT WAS BUILT IN 1979, THE SKYSCRAPER **NECOM HOUSE** WAS THE TALLEST BUILDING IN WEST AFRICA.

SPORT ALSO PLAYS AN IMPORTANT ROLE IN **LAGOS**. THE POPULARITY AND SPORTING SKILLS OF ACE FOOTBALLER TESLIM BALOGUN, UNITED LAGOS FOOTBALL FANS - A STADIUM IN HIS HONOUR WAS FINISHED IN 2007. THE CITY'S NATIONAL STADIUM HAS HOSTED THE AFRICAN CUP OF NATIONS AS WELL AS OTHER MAJOR EVENTS.

EVERY **LAGOSIAN** PLAYS AN IMPORTANT ROLE IN DEVELOPING AND SUSTAINING COMMUNITIES AND PUBLIC SERVICES. AND THE ECONOMY IS FROM THE **STOCK EXCHANGE** ESTABLISHED IN LAGOS TO BUOYING THE ECONOMY IN OTHER WAYS.

... SUCH AS SHOPPING IN THE **MARKETS,** BUZZING WITH PEOPLE, GOODS, BARGAINS AND FRESH FOOD. NO SELL-BY DATES AND NO FIXED PRICES – HAGGLE! YOU CAN GET WHATEVER YOU WANT: EVERYONE IS SELLING OR BUYING. **IDUMOTA** IS ONE OF THE OLDEST CITY MARKETS.

THE CITY IS AN EXCITING PLACE TO BE – THOUGH IT'S TRUE THAT WE SUFFER FROM RAMPANT POWER OUTAGES. BUT WITH THEIR GENERATORS, CANDLES, LAMPS AND LANTERNS, LAGOS'S PEOPLE WILL NOT BOW TO DARKNESS!

I'VE TOLD YOU SOME OF OUR LAGOS'S STORY, BUT SINCE THE 19TH CENTURY, THE **WHITE CAP CHIEFS** HAVE BEEN THE CUSTODIANS OF THE ORAL HISTORY OF THE CITY, KNOWLEDGE WHICH IS PASSED FROM GENERATION TO GENERATION.

© Tayo Fatunla

Text 2: GraceLand

by Chris Abani (2004)

Novelist and poet Chris Abani is one of a new generation of Nigerian writers working to convey to English-speaking readers the experience of those raised in this troubled African nation. After his first novel, "Masters of the Board", was published when he was only 16, Abani was thrown in jail for six months as the novel was deemed too political. After subsequently being imprisoned twice more for his political views, Abani was able to escape to the UK in 1991. Since 2001 he has lived in exile in the US.

Chris Abani's novel GraceLand tells the story of 14-year-old Elvis's struggle to survive in the impoverished and crime-ridden ghettos of Lagos. Having lost his mother to cancer at a young age, he now lives with his abusive father. Elvis tries to eke out a living as an Elvis Presley impersonator in order to escape the harsh environment of the slum. The two extracts here are taken from the beginning of the story.

ONE

This is the kola nut. This seed is a star. This star is life.
This star is us.

5 *The Igbo hold the kola nut to be sacred, offering it at every gathering*
and to every visitor, as a blessing, as refreshment, or to seal a covenant.
The prayer that precedes the breaking and sharing of the nut is: He
who brings kola, brings life.

Lagos, 1983

10 Elvis stood by the open window. Outside: heavy rain. He jammed
the wooden shutter open with an old radio battery, against the wind.
The storm drowned the tinny sound of the portable radio on the
table. He felt claustrophobic, fingers gripping the iron of the rusty
metal protector. It was cool on his lips, chin and forehead as he
15 pressed his face against it.

Across the street stood the foundations of a building; the floor
and pillars wore green mold from repeated rains. Between the
pillars, a woman had erected a buka, no more than a rickety lean-to
made of sheets of corrugated iron roofing and plastic held together
20 by hope. On dry evenings, the smell of fried yam and dodo wafted

---

3 **kola nut** fruit of the kola tree, important part of Nigerian Igbo cultural traditions –
5 **Igbo** ethnic group living in southeastern Nigeria – 6 **to seal** *besiegeln, beschließen* –
6 **covenant** [ˈkʌvənənt] agreement, contract – 10 **to jam** to fix sth so it cannot
close – 12 **tinny** low quality – 18 **buka** small stall or kiosk selling food – 20 **yam** sweet
potato – 20 **dodo** fried plantain, Nigerian dish

from it into his room, teasing his hunger. But today the fire grate was wet and all the soot had been washed away.

As swiftly as it started, the deluge abated, becoming a faint drizzle. Water, thick with sediment, ran down the rust-colored iron roofs, overflowing basins and drums set out to collect it. Taps stood in yards, forlorn and lonely, their curved spouts, like metal beaks, dripping rainwater. Naked children exploded out of grey wet houses, slipping and splaying in the mud, chased by shouts of parents trying to get them ready for school.

The rain had cleared the oppressive heat that had already dropped like a blanket over Lagos; but the smell of garbage from refuse dumps, unflushed toilets and stale bodies was still overwhelming. Elvis turned from the window, dropping the threadbare curtain. Today was his sixteenth birthday, and as with all the others, it would pass uncelebrated. It had been that way since his mother died eight years before. He used to think that celebrating his birthday was too painful for his father, a constant reminder of his loss. But Elvis had since come to the conclusion that his father was simply self-centered. The least I should do is get some more sleep, he thought, sitting on the bed. But the sun stabbed through the thin fabric, bathing the room in sterile light. The radio played Bob Marley's "Natural Mystic," and he sang along, the tune familiar.

"There's a natural mystic blowing through the air / If you listen carefully now you will hear …" His voice trailed off as he realized he did not know all the words, and he settled for humming to the song as he listened to the sounds of the city waking up: tin buckets scraping, the sound of babies crying, infants yelling for food and people hurrying but getting nowhere.

---

1 **grate** *here*: *Grillrost, Feuerrost* – 3 **deluge** [ˈdeljuːdʒ] very heavy rain – 3 **to abate** to become less – 12 **stale** *here*: not washed, dirty – 13 **threadbare** old, well-worn – 26 **tin bucket** *Blecheimer*

Next door someone was playing highlife music on a radio that was not tuned properly. The faster-tempoed highlife distracted him from Bob Marley, irritating him. He knew the highlife tune well, "Ije Enu" by Celestine Ukwu. Abandoning Bob Marley, he sang along:

"Ije enu, bun a ndi n'kwa n'kwa ndi n'wuli n'wuli, eh …"

On the road outside, two women bickered. In the distance, the sounds of molue conductors competing for customers carried:

"Yaba! Yaba! Straight!"

"Oshodi! Oshodi! Enter quickly!"

Elvis looked around his room. *Jesus Can Save* and *Nigerian Eagles* almanacs hung from stained walls that had not seen a coat of paint in years. A magazine cutting of a BMW was coming off the far wall, its end flapping mockingly. The bare cement floor was a cracked and pitted lunar landscape. A piece of wood, supported at both ends by cinder blocks, served as a bookshelf. On it were arranged his few books each volume falling apart from years of use.

By the window was a dust-coated desk, and next to it a folding metal chair, brown and crisp with rust. The single camping cot he lay on was sunk in the center and the water-thin mattress offered as much comfort as a raffia mat. A wooden bar secured diagonally between two corners of the room served as a closet.

There was a loud knock, and as Elvis gathered the folds of his loincloth around his waist to get up, the lappa, once beautiful but now hole-ridden, caught on the edge of the bed, ripping a curse from him. The book he had fallen asleep reading, Ralph Ellison's *Invisible Man*, fell from his side to the floor, the old paperback cracking at the spine, falling neatly into two halves as precisely as if sliced by a sword.

---

1 **highlife** Ghanaian style of music – 4 **Celestine Ukwu** (1940–1977) Nigerian Igbo musician – 11 **almanac** annual calendar – 15 **cinder block** *Betonstein* – 18 **camping cot** camp bed – 20 **raffia mat** *Bastmatte* – 26 **Invisible Man** novel by R. Ellison addressing some of the issues facing African Americans in the early twentieth century

"Elvis! Elvis! Wake up. It's past six in de morning and all your mates are out dere looking for work," his father, Sunday, said.

"What work, sir? I have a job."

"Dancing is no job. We all dance in de bar on Saturday. Open dis
5 bloody door!" Sunday shouted.

Elvis opened the door and eyed him. The desire to drive his fist through his father's face was old and overwhelming.

"I'll just wash, then go," he mumbled, shuffling past Sunday, heading for the backyard, passing Jagua Rigogo, who stood in the
10 middle of the backyard cleaning his teeth with a chewing-stick, preparing for his morning ablutions and the clients who would soon start arriving to consult him on spiritual matters. He reached out and squeezed Elvis's arm as he passed. Elvis turned to him, opening his mouth to speak.

15 "Before you speak, my friend, remember, a spiritual man contain his anger. Angry words are like slap in de face."

Elvis took in Jagua's dreadlocks, gathered behind him in a long ponytail by a twisted tennis headband, and the distant red glare of his eyes. He didn't have his python with him, and Elvis wondered
20 where it was. Probably asleep in the cot Jagua had salvaged from one of the city dumps, and which sat in the corner of his room. Merlin, his python, slept in it, comfortable as any baby.

"Jagua. I …" Elvis began, then stopped.

Jagua smiled, mistaking Elvis's resignation for control. "Dat's de
25 way," he said.

Elvis just sighed and silently fetched water from the iron drum sunning in a corner of the yard. He snatched his towel off the line and entered the bathroom, trying not to touch the slime-covered walls and the used sanitary pad in the corner. How did they come
30 to this? he wondered. Just two years ago they lived in a small town

---

11 **ablutions** (*pl, hum*) washing oneself – 20 **to salvage** to save, to rescue – 24 **Dat's** (*Nigerian dialect*) That's

and his father had a good job and was on the cusp of winning an election. Now they lived in a slum in Lagos. Closing his eyes, he rushed through his morning toilet. On his way back inside to get dressed, he passed his father in the corridor again.

"Are you still here?"

Elvis opened his mouth to answer but thought better of it.

The road outside their tenement was waterlogged and the dirt had been whipped into a muddy brown froth that looked like chocolate frosting. Someone had laid out short planks to carve a path through the sludge. Probably Joshua Bandele-Thomas, Elvis thought. Joshua was the eccentric who lived next door and spent his days pretending to be a surveyor.

Elvis and his father lived at the left edge of the swamp city of Maroko, and their short street soon ran into a plank walkway that meandered through the rest of the suspended city. Even with the planks, the going was slow, as he often had to wait for people coming in the opposite direction to pass; the planks were that narrow.

While he waited, Elvis stared into the muddy puddles imagining what life, if any, was trying to crawl its way out. His face, reflected back at him, seemed to belong to a stranger, floating there like a ghostly head in a comic book. His hair was closely cropped, almost shaved clean. His eyebrows were two perfect arcs, as though they had been shaped in a salon. His dark eyes looked tired, the whites flecked with red. He parted his full lips and tried a smile on his reflection, and his reflection snarled back. Shit, he thought, I look like shit. As he sloshed to the bus stop, one thought repeated in his mind: What do I have to do with all this?

---

1 **be on the cusp of sth** (*phrase*) to be just about to – 7 **tenement** [ˈtenəmənt] flat, apartment – 7 **waterlogged** flooded, full of water – 10 **sludge** *(Abwasser)Schlamm* – 12 **surveyor** sb whose job it is to measure and record features of areas of land – 13 **swamp city of Maroko** (or Makoko) area of Lagos built on stilts along the lagoon, a huge slum with bad infrastructure

Sitting on the crowded bus, he thought his father might be right; this was no way to live. He was broke all the time, making next to nothing as a street performer. He needed a better job with a regular income. He pulled a book from his backpack and tried to read. It was his current inspirational tome, a well-thumbed copy of Rilke's *Letters to a Young Poet*. He read books for different reasons and had them everywhere he was: one in his backpack, which he called his on-the-road book, usually one that held an inspirational message for him; one by his bed; and one he kept tucked in the hole in the wall in the toilet for those cool evenings when a gentle breeze actually made the smell there bearable enough to stay and read. He opened the book and tried to read, sitting back as far as he could in the narrow seat. He hated the way he was being pressed against the metal side by the heavyset woman sitting next to him, one ample buttock on the seat, the other hanging in the aisle, supported against a standing stranger's leg. Elvis shifted, careful of the loose metal spring poking up through the torn plastic of the seat cover. Giving up on reading, he let his mind drift as he stared at the city, half slum, half paradise. How could a place be so ugly and violent yet beautiful at the same time? he wondered.

He hadn't known about the poverty and violence of Lagos until he arrived. It was as if people conspired with the city to weave a web of silence around its unsavory parts. People who didn't live in Lagos only saw postcards of skyscrapers, sweeping flyovers, beaches and hotels. And those who did, when they returned to their ancestral small towns at Christmas, wore designer clothes and threw money around. They breezed in, lived an expensive whirlwind life, and then left after a couple of weeks, to go back to their ghetto lives.

---

5 tome (*hum*) (large) book – **22 to weave** (wove, woven) *weben* – **23 unsavory** [ʌnˈseɪvəri] disgusting, nasty

But for one brilliant moment, they dazzled: the women in flashy clothes, makeup and handbags that matched their shoes, daring to smoke in public and drink beer straight from the bottle; and the men, sharp dressers who did not rat on you to your parents if they caught you smoking. They let you take sips of their beer and shoved a few naira into your shirt pocket.

Lagos did have its fair share of rich people and fancy neighborhoods, though, and since arriving he had found that one-third of the city seemed transplanted from the rich suburbs of the west. There were beautiful brownstones set in well-landscaped yards, sprawling Spanish-style haciendas in brilliant white and ocher, elegant Frank Lloyd Wright-styled buildings and cars that were new and foreign. Name it and Lagos had a copy of it, earning it the nickname "One Copy." Elvis had read a newspaper editorial that stated, rather proudly, that Nigeria had a higher percentage of millionaires—in dollars, not local currency—than nearly any other country in the world, and most of them lived and conducted their business in Lagos. The editorial failed to mention that their wealth had been made over the years with the help of crooked politicians, criminal soldiers, bent contractors, and greedy oil-company executives. Or that Nigeria also had a higher percentage of poor people than nearly any other country in the world. What was it his father had said about statistics?

"If you have it, flaunt it; if you don't, flaunt statistics."

He had been fourteen when he arrived in Lagos two years before, miserable and unable to fit into school, where his small-town thinking and accent marked him. The differences did not seem that obvious, but they were glaring to the other kids—he'd never played

---

1 **to dazzle** *here*: to amaze, to impress – 6 **naira** Nigerian currency – 10 **brownstone** house built of reddish-brown stone – 11 **hacienda** [ˌhasɪˈendə] (Spanish) large house or estate – 19 **crooked** *here*: corrupt – 20 **bent contractor** *korrupte Vertragspartner* – 24 **to flaunt** to show sth in public

cricket at school, his experience of the movies had been with old dubbed-over silents and the Americanisms he knew were old and outdated. Where the other kids used slang like "cool" and "hip," he was limited to cowboy lingo like "shucks" and "yup" and "darn those rustlers."

So he cut school, spending long periods of time on a deserted beach, not too far from the ghetto of Maroko where they lived. He practiced his dance routines for hours to the sound of his little radio. At first the sand slowed him down, making his movements jerky. But he persevered until his moves appeared effortless. Subsequently, when he danced on smooth surfaces, he seemed to float. The beach was also refuge to the homeless beggars moved on by the police; always polite, they offered to share their "tickets to paradise." Elvis always refused the marijuana, but the smell hung in the hot air, and it soon became difficult to engage fully with the reality around him.

A man arguing loudly in the back of the bus intruded on his thoughts and reminded Elvis of his first molue ride. Molues were buses unique to Lagos, and only that place could have devised such a hybrid vehicle, its "magic" the only thing keeping it from falling apart. The cab of the bus was imported from Britain, one of the Bedford series. The chassis of the body came from surplus Japanese army trucks trashed after the Second World War. The body of the coach was built from scraps of broken cars and discarded roofing sheets—anything that could be beaten into shape or otherwise fashioned. The finished product, with two black stripes running down a canary body, looked like a roughly hammered yellow sardine tin.

---

5 **rustler** sb who steals animals – 10 **jerky** not fluent or smooth – 22 **surplus** (*adj*) more than needed, too much – 24 **roofing sheet** *Dachabdeckung*

The buses had a full capacity of forty-nine sitting and nine standing, but often held sixty and twenty. People hung off the sides and out of the doors. Some even stood on the back bumpers and held on to the roof rack. The buses wove through the dense traffic so fast they threw the passengers about, and caused those hanging on to sway dangerously. An old man on the bus had told him that the spirits of the road danced around the buses trying to pluck plump offerings, retribution for the sacrilege of the road, which apparently, when it was built, had severed them from their roots, leaving them trapped in an urban chaos that was frightening and confusing. Elvis never knew whether these spirits inhabited a particular road or all roads, or what they looked like. But the old man's story sounded so plausible it had stayed with him. Elvis yawned, closed his eyes and rested his head on the cool metal side. Suddenly a man in the front got up, rapped his knuckles noisily on the roof of the bus and cleared his throat.

"Good morning, ladies and gentlemen."

His voice had a curious ring to it.

"We get new product for sale today call Pracetmol. It cures all pains, aches and fever caused in de body. If you look at de package, you will see dat de expiry date is December eighty-three. Dis is a new drug from de white people's labs and plenty research done go into it. It is manufacture in Yugoslavia. In dat country dey call it narcotics and it is costing plenty money. We in Star Advertising Agency with head office in Orile Lagos have been choose by de makers to promote dis drug in Nigeria. Today you can obtain your copy at cheap rate from me. Due to and because of advert purpose, dis packet containing twenty tablet is costing only one naira. If you

---

4 **to weave** (wove, weaved) *here*: to move – 8 **sacrilege** [ˈsækrɪlɪdʒ] *Frevel* – 15 **knuckle** joint of a finger – 21 **expiry date** date after which sth should not be used – 24 **narcotic** *Betäubungsmittel*

check any chemist it is costing three naira dere. Buy your own now, for mama, papa and childrens too …"

Elvis tried to tune out the voice of the drug vendor but could not. Luckily the vendor got off at the next stop and Elvis watched him cross the road and hop onto a bus going the opposite way, relieved that he didn't have to listen to him all the way to Iddoh Park. Sitting back, Elvis closed his eyes again, and just as he drifted off, the insistent calling of a mobile preacher woke him. The preacher was wearing a grimy, threadbare white robe and unkempt dreadlocks; he had a Bible in one hand, and in the other a huge bell with which he punctuated his ravings. He must have gotten on when the drug vendor got off.

"Repent, I say. I am a voice crying out in de wilderness. Repent and come unto de Lord before it becomes too late. I saw a vision from de Lord and he did reveal many things to me. Listen—I say, listen," he said, reinforcing his ranting with loud and generous peals from his bell. "De Lord says de only road to salvation lies in de Yahweh Adonai Latter Day Prophetic Spiritual and Messianic Church of God and His Blessed Son Jesus of Mount Carmel. Amen. Listen, brethren, I am de representation of dis wonderful Church of God and I call on all who will be saved from damnation to visit us on Sundays near Ojo bus stop and see miracles happen. Witness de power of prayer, de lame shall walk and de blind see. Listen …"

Elvis couldn't take any more and got off at the Bar Beach stop. It was a nice day, not too hot, with a nice breeze coming off the ocean, and he thought he might make some money off white expatriates and the odd tourist tanning on the beach. They were always surprised and pleased to see an Elvis impersonator here, particularly

---

9 **grimy** dirty – 11 **to punctuate** to interrupt – 11 **ravings** (*pl*) mad or strange talk –
16 **ranting** angry and violent talk – 26 **expatriate** [ekˈspætriət] sb who does not live in
their home country

the Americans, who were often quite generous. He crossed the hot
sand of the beach that abutted the Hilton Hotel. As he walked
toward the makeshift raffia changing stalls, he noted who was there.

Sprawled on a deck chair was a heavyset man with a gargantuan

5 stomach on which sat an open book. The sun was burning the skin
around it and Elvis wondered if the resulting white patch would
contain any of the text. A harried-looking woman with red hair and
skin reddening to match chased after three excited children, ranging
from around five to nine. In her hand was a white smudge of

10 sunscreen, and with her distracted expression, she looked as though
she suddenly realized she was holding a bodily secretion. Her
husband (if he was her husband) was dozing on another deck chair,
which was missing a leg. With every snore it tottered precariously
but, defying the laws of physics, remained upright. An elderly couple

15 stood looking out to the horizon, hands cupped against the glare of
sun on water as though looking for their lost youth.

Meager pickings, he thought, as he ducked into a stall and shed
his street clothes. He slipped into the white shirt and trousers, pulled
on the socks and canvas shoes, and jammed the wig down on his

20 head. He couldn't see himself properly in the small pocket mirror
he carried. In Iddoh Park, his usual spot, he had come to rely on the
glass shop fronts for his reflection. He hoped he looked fine.

[…]

---

2 **to abut** to share a border with sth – 4 **gargantuan** [gɑːrˈgæntʃuən] very big, gigantic –
7 **harried** stressed, overworked – 9 **smudge** dirty mark – 13 **to totter** to shake, to tremble

TWO

We worship in different ways. With wine, the flow of worldly
sweetness; with alligator pepper seeds, the hot and painful trials;
with nzu, the sign of peace; with water, the blessing of the
holy spirit; with blood, the essence of all life; with food, to fill the
hunger of gods; with prayers, to allay the wrath of demons.
But greatest of all this, is the offering of kola in communion,
the soul calling unto life.

The Eucharistic qualities of the kola-nut ritual are clear. There are
close parallels to Catholicism, as there seems to be some kind of
transubstantiation involved in the kolanut ceremony, similar to the
communion wafer in the Catholic ritual of mass. There is the invocation
of a supreme deity, the reference to the kola nut as representative of life
and by association, the implication that the consumption of one was
equal to that of the other.

Afikpo, 1972

Elvis had no idea why his father had summoned him to the backyard,
away from the toy fire engine he was playing with. He had no idea
why he had been asked to strip down to his underwear, or why Uncle
Joseph first strapped a grass skirt on him and then began to paint
strange designs in red and white dye all over his body. But he was
five years old, and had learned not only that no one explained much
to him, but that it was safest not to ask. Uncle Joseph had a habit of
expressing his impatience in slaps.

---

3 **alligator pepper** West African spice – 6 **to allay** to calm down, to quiet – 6 **wrath** [ræθ]
Zorn – 11 **transubstantiation** *religiöse Wandlung* – 12 **invocation** way of calling upon a
spirit or a god – 13 **deity** [ˈdiːəti] god or goddess

His mother, Beatrice, stood in the shadows, leaning on a door-frame for support. She was ill and had been for a while. Whatever was going on must be important, Elvis thought, if she had gotten out of bed for it. She had a sudden coughing bout and would have fallen over had Aunt Felicia not caught her and led her back in.

"Mommy! Mommy!" Elvis called, struggling to get to her.

"Stand still," Sunday said, pulling him roughly by the arm. He stumbled, but steadied himself against his uncle. Near tears, he watched Beatrice retreat into the house. He looked around for Oye, but she was nowhere to be found. Instead he saw his teenage cousins, Innocent and Godfrey, and a gaggle of other boys ranging from ten to nineteen. This group was made up of young men from the neighboring hamlets that had come to welcome Elvis on his first step to manhood as dictated by tradition, and as part of the ritual they would form a retinue of singers. The truth was, they were only there because they hoped that they would all be treated to good food and plenty to drink. Sunday noticed Elvis's attention straying and realized that he was looking for his mother and grandmother.

"It is time to cut your apron strings," he said to Elvis. "Dis is about being a man. No women allowed."

"Easy, Sunday," Joseph said.

"Easy what? Dis is why he has to learn early how to be a man, you know?"

"I know, but easy."

Elvis stood still throughout the exchange as Joseph continued to paint.

"Eh, Joseph, I have some White Horse whiskey, let me bring it?"

"You need to ask?" Joseph replied with a chuckle.

Sunday got up and went in the house to fetch the whiskey from his private hoard in his bedroom. From the house came the quiet

---

4 **bout** *here*: attack, fit – 11 **gaggle** group

protest of Elvis Presley's "Return to Sender" played at a low volume.
As soon as Sunday was gone, Elvis started asking questions.

"What is happening?"

"Today, Elvis, you are going to kill your first eagle."

"But I'm too little."

"Don't worry," Uncle Joseph said, laughing.

"But why must I kill the eagle?"

"It is de first step into manhood for you. When you are older, de
next step is to kill a goat, and den from dere we begin your manhood
rites. But dis is de first step."

Sunday returned shortly with the whiskey and two shot glasses.
He sat down with a grunt and opened the bottle. Holding it over
the ground, he poured a libation, while Joseph responded at
appropriate moments. Joseph took the proffered shot glass and
downed the whiskey in one gulp, snapping the empty glass out to
his side, allowing any errant drops to water the ground. He grunted
and grimaced.

"Ah, Sunday, dat na good brew dere. Pour me anoder."

"Don't finish my good whiskey. Dis stuff is not kaikai."

When Joseph finished painting Elvis, he sent his son Godfrey out
to summon the male elders. While he was gone, Joseph handed Elvis
a small homemade bow with an arrow strung in it. On the end of
the arrow, pierced through its side, was a chick. It was still alive and
it chirped sadly. There was a line of blood from its beak that ran into
the yellow down around its neck. The blood was beginning to
harden and stiffen the feathers into a red necktie.

"It is alive," Elvis said.

"Of course it is. You just shot it," Joseph replied.

"I didn't."

---

12 **grunt** deep sound – 13 **libation** drink poured out as an offering to a deity – 18 **brew**
drink – 19 **kaikai** (*NPidgin*) home-made gin – 22 **bow and arrow** *Pfeil und Bogen* –
26 **necktie** band worn around the neck

"You did," Sunday said.

"Is this an eagle chick?" Elvis asked.

Joseph laughed. "Elvis, you funny. No, it is chicken, eagle is too expensive."

Elvis stood there holding the bow and arrow, with the helpless chick as far away from him as possible. He did not want the blood touching him. He tried not to make eye contact with the dying bird. When the old men assembled, Sunday passed the whiskey around and the men took swigs straight from the bottle.

"Do we have a kill?" they asked in Igbo, all speaking as one.

"Yes, we have a kill," Joseph replied.

"Was it a good kill?" the old men asked.

"Yes," Sunday answered.

"The father cannot speak," the old men said.

"Yes," Joseph said.

"Where is the kill?"

Joseph pointed and Elvis stepped forward. The old men smiled and looked at one another.

"In our day it was a real eagle."

"Let's just get on with it," Sunday said.

The old men glowered at him. Then, one by one, they walked up to Elvis and blew chalk powder in his face. They anointed his head with oil and, taking the bow and arrow from him and passing it to Joseph, they spat in his palms and muttered a blessing for him. Then they walked out of the compound.

Innocent, at fifteen, was Elvis's eldest cousin. Elvis knew that Innocent had been a boy soldier in the civil war that ended two years before and that when Innocent slept over at Elvis's house, he woke up in the middle of the night, screaming. Oye told him that Innocent screamed because the ghosts of those he had killed in the war were tormenting him, and if he, Elvis, didn't behave, Innocent's ghosts

---

31 **to torment** to torture, to make sb suffer

would torment him too. Other than the war story, Innocent and Godfrey, who was thirteen, were virtually strangers to Elvis. He admired them from a distance with their towering Afros and platform shoes, but as teenagers they didn't have much to do with him.

Innocent bent and lifted Elvis up onto his shoulders. He felt very grown-up sitting up there, seeing the world from that high. Uncle Joseph handed the bow back to Elvis and they followed the old men out of the compound, accompanied by the group of young men, who now joined the procession, singing.

They followed the old men up the road, singing the praises of Elvis as a great warrior and hunter. The road headed away from the square, toward the farms and ritual spaces. It was unpaved and lined by trees Elvis knew simply as bush mango trees. They grew in straight lines. He once asked Oye how come wild trees could grow in such a straight line.

"They don't, laddie," she said. "In tha olden days, criminals and murderers were buried alive, standing up. A flowering stake was driven through their heads and they became the trees. Tha's why tha fruit is so sweet."

She cackled at his horrified expression. Beatrice had intervened.

"Mama! He is only five."

"Children are never too young to hear tha truth. You know why tha criminals were killed tha' way? Redemption. In death they were given a chance to be useful, to feed fruit-bearing trees. Do you understand?"

Elvis shook his head.

"Don't worry, someday you will."

But Elvis couldn't walk past the trees without feeling the ghosts of the criminals reaching out to him, and neither could he eat the tasty fruit. High up on Innocent's shoulders, he felt the leaves brush

---

13 **unpaved** *unbefestigt, ungepflastert* – 18 **stake** stick, pole

his face like hungry fingers, and he was really glad when the old men turned off the road and into the bush. They soon came upon a huge iroko tree that served as the clan shrine. The old men stopped and, taking the bow and arrow from Elvis, approached the tree. They freed the chick, tying it upside down to a branch next to others that were in several stages of decay. They hung like grotesque ornaments on a Christmas tree. The old men plucked a tail feather from the bird and stuck it in Elvis's hair. They cut the tree bark and, dipping their fingers in the sap, traced patterns on his face. And then it was over. Sunday picked Elvis up and held him close to the decaying birds. Elvis turned away from the smell.

"Don't turn away from death. We must face it. We are men,'" Sunday said.

Elvis turned to him, tears brimming.

"But it stinks."

"So does life, boy. So does life," Joseph said. "Come, Sunday, leave your son to join his mates. He is a man now. Come, we still have to finish dat whiskey."

Sunday nodded. He looked at Elvis for a long moment before putting him down.

Turning to Innocent and Godfrey, he told them to watch over their cousin, and then he left with Joseph. The group of singing boys followed them, intent on joining in on any festivities. Innocent picked Elvis up and carried him on his shoulders as they walked back to the house. He stopped at a kiosk just outside the compound.

"Why are we stopping?" Godfrey asked.

"Ah Elvis done taste him first blood, so as a man, he must drink with men," Innocent replied.

Ordering beers for himself and Godfrey, he opened up a cold bottle of Fanta for Elvis.

---

3 **clan shrine** holy place where a group of families gathers to pray – 9 **sap** liquid from a tree – 10 **to decay** [dɪˈkeɪ] to rot, to decompose

"How you dey?" Innocent asked him.

"I was afraid," Elvis replied.

"Dat's how dese things are. De trials of dis world things come as surprise, so you must have a warrior's heart to withstand dem. Dat's why your papa no tell you about today. You understand?" Innocent said.

Elvis shook his head and took a sip from his soda.

"Leave him. He is a child," Godfrey said. "Dere is time for such talk later."

Innocent nodded and took a swig of beer. Sitting on the counter in his grass skirt, drinking his Fanta and watching Godfrey and Innocent tease the girl behind the counter, Elvis felt like a man.

© Chris Abani

Text 3: A Dynasty of Album Cover Art

by Lemi Ghariokwu (Granta Magazine, 2013)

Lemi Ghariokwu is an award-wining and self-taught illustrator and artist from Lagos who received his big break in 1974 when a journalist
happened to see some of his drawings and set up a meeting with Fela Kuti, the pioneer of Afrobeat (a genre of music that mixes elements of West African musical styles with American jazz, soul and funk influences). Lemi went on to design 26 album covers for Fela Kuti, bold and highly visual designs that gave life to Fela's lyrics.

Over the course of his career Lemi has designed over 2,000 album covers for musicians around the globe. Since 2002 his work has regularly been exhibited internationally.

In this essay Lemi tells the story behind some of his album cover designs for Fela Kuti.

As a youngster and aspiring artist in the early 1970s, I learnt a lot from attending art exhibitions and visiting private studios and galleries in Lagos. It was a ritual for me to flip through newspapers eagerly to check out the cartoon page where the artists reign
5 supreme with their take on socio-political issues in the country. My other pastime was to check out the street sign-writers and their organic form of art. The minibuses in Lagos always had philosophical slogans written on them.

In Nigeria, everyday life is noted not so much for the abundance
10 of technology as for the fact that so much of it does not function. The country's political rulers are not satisfying the needs of the people and are interested primarily in enriching themselves. A new enemy has also arisen in Nigeria – insecurity has intensified due to kidnapping and terrorist extremism. Yet despite the despair, the
15 underlying attitude has remained irrepressibly optimistic. In the last three decades or more, a couple of artists have started using the tools at their disposal to analyse political developments. Fela Anikulapo-Kuti was one major artist; with his Afrobeat music, he challenged the forces of repression and corruption in governance in the state
20 of Nigeria. He suffered great consequences but never gave up the fight till his death.

---

1 **aspiring** [əˈspaɪ̯ə-ɪŋ] ambitious – 4 **to reign** to rule – 6 **pastime** hobby, leisure activity –
9 **abundance** large amount of sth, wealth – 17 **Fela Anikulapo-Kuti** (1938–1997) known
as Fela Kuti, Nigerian multi-instrumentalist, composer and musician, pioneer of Afrobeat
music

In 1974, I earned Fela's trust and friendship through my acquaintanceship with the journalist Babatunde Harrison. Fela had just experienced his first beating and incarceration by the police and this gruesome experience inspired the hit song 'Alagbon Close', which was the first cover I designed. Having listened ardently to recountings of the harrowing experience from the man himself and having been privy to the stages of the composition of the tune, the cover was a fait accompli. It actually started with a drawing of Fela I had in my portfolio prior to my chance meeting with 'Tunde Harrison, which showed the musician dancing on a mishmash of mud and rubbish. The final design of 'Alagbon Close's' cover showed Fela's 'Kalakuta Republic' in the background standing solidly on the left and Alagbon Close jailhouse on the right, a broken chain leading from the walls of the jail, half of which is still attached to Fela's left wrist as he dances triumphantly over a capsizing police patrol boat and is helped, in effect, by a prodigious whale.

---

3 **incarceration** imprisonment – 5 **ardently** passionately – 8 **fait accompli** [ˌfeɪtəkɑːmˈpliː] *vollendete Tatsache* – 12 **Kalakuta Republic** Fela Kuti's house – 13 **jailhouse** jail, prison – 15 **to capsize** to turn over in water (of a boat) – 16 **prodigious** [prəˈdɪdʒəs] enormous, great

The next two album covers for *No Bread* and *Kalakuta Show* followed the tow of Fela's vitriolic statements on vinyl. *No Bread* was an elaborate oil painting; portraying a mélange of social ills plaguing a developing nation; the cover forespoke of the doom to come. This cover took the best of two weeks and a trip to 'cloud nine' to achieve. Fela had insisted I try out a concoction of *igbo* (marijuana) to 'elevate' my talent. Not wanting to let my great friend down, I tried the herb and the resultant effect was superb, but being a teetotaller and someone with a mind of his own, I learned to be myself and thereafter tune into the right frequency. *Kalakuta Show* is another oil painting, this time illustrating the arrogant sacking of the 'Republic' in another Fela-versus-Police drama, featuring a portrait of Fela with the smoking Kalakuta Republic in the background, while Fela, his aides and his radical lawyer are hotly pursued by a baton-wielding policeman!

My association and friendship with the maverick was very cordial. I was treated like a son, friend, adviser and comrade by the Afrobeat legend. I was a travelling companion, sharing the great ideology of Pan-Africanism on some of the trips across the West African coast. Between 1974 and 1993 I designed twenty-six album covers for his music career.

---

3 **ills** (*pl*) problems, misfortunes – 5 **cloud nine** a feeling of great happiness – 6 **concoction** combination, mixture – 8 **teetotaller** [ˌtiːˈtoʊtələ˞] person who doesn't drink alcohol (in this case does not use any addictive substances) – 16 **maverick** unorthodox person – 17 **cordial** friendly, warm

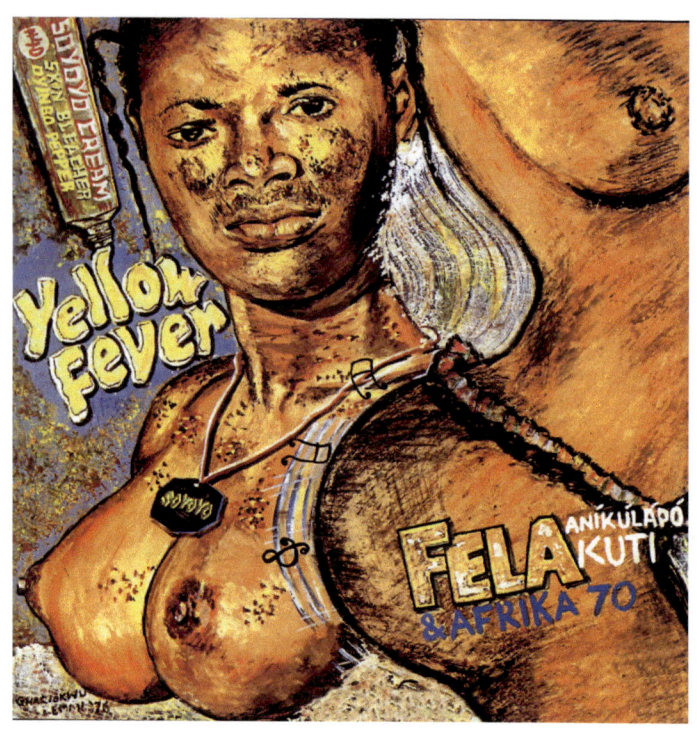

I designed the *Yellow Fever* cover in 1976. The song is an admonition to African women who are fond of using bleaching creams to lighten their dark skin tone, and I did use a model to express visually what Fela has orally illustrated in the song. Points of emphasis include the bad effect the bleach has on the face and bum. My life model was a girl named Kokor who was a member of the household at Kalakuta Republic. I decided it was going to be a straight-in-your-face image of misinformed African beauty. Fela had already expressed disgust at the belief that skin lightening enhances African beauty. I showcased a typical 'offending' cream in the top-left corner of my cover art. '*Soyoyo* Cream Skin Bleacher' was actually my own creation. The word *soyoyo* is a Yoruba expression for 'bright and glow'! I painted in the price tag of 40 naira which was high end for a cream, and yet so harmful to beauty and the psyche of African women. Fela reacted very positively when I submitted this cover for his approval and in his characteristic manner said glowingly 'Goddamn!', wittily adding 'Lemi is a mutherfucker me-e-n!' just to round up.

In 1976, the then-military government in Nigeria had instructed soldiers to horsewhip erring drivers on the highway. The soldiers carried out this order without impunity and with a fervour reminiscent of zombies. That was why, having been severally harassed by military personnel, Fela came up with the idea to compose 'Zombie'. Everyone, including some military personnel from the nearby Albati Barracks, fell in love with the catchy rhythm and martial tempo, which galvanized the dancers, who wouldn't let the song end. Fela's saucy reprise of the Army Bugle call and horn riff got them jumping and whooping with the release of being able to mock oppressors they both feared and despised. The song became an anthem of protest for people, which was chanted under their breath anytime they felt oppressed by military personnel.

---

1 **admonition** warning – 12 **Yoruba** ethnic group inhabiting western Africa – 16 **wittily** amusingly – 21 **reminiscent of** like – 25 **to galvanize** to stimulate – 28 **to despise** to strongly dislike

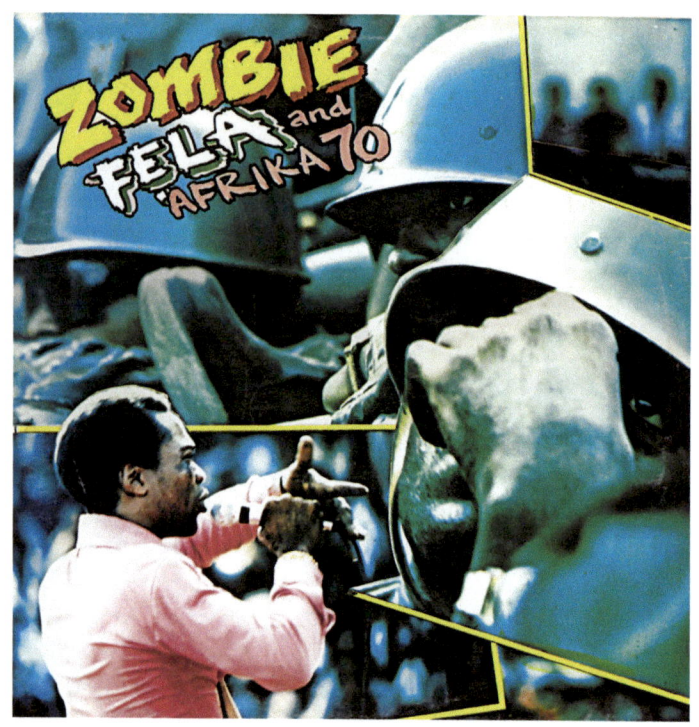

When the time came to create the cover art for this landmark song, I found myself unable to focus on the right idea initially. The breakthrough came right on time one Kalakuta morning just as Fela was asking how the sleeve was coming along. Tunde Kuboye, the photographer, film-maker, jazz musician husband of Fela's niece, Frances, walked in with a bunch of his photographs taken at that year's Independence Day military parade at Tafawa Balewa Square in central Lagos. With Tunde's permission, I selected ten military images, and a few of Fela. I was set on making a graphic collage. Back in my studio I laid a cardboard mat on my drawing board and edited Tunde's ten shots down to four. I was feeling like a shaman, and as I put them down, the pictures just dropped into a position reminiscent of an Ifa divination . . . subconsciously! Not wanting to take any chances, I fixed the pictures down with masking tape, then traced their position in pencil. I overlapped the photos and cut and pasted them down. Then, using a hard paintbrush and thick poster colour paint, I wrote, in freehand, the album title, Fela's name and his band directly over the picture, outlining the result with a Rotring pen. Finally, I added the shadows.

The sleeve was an instant hit at Kalakuta, in Nigeria, Africa and around the world. It led new listeners to wonder what lay on the vinyl inside. For the initiated, it told the story of life under an oppressive military dictatorship – and what it takes to come through it feeling that you're still somehow in command of your destiny.

---

11 **shaman** a person who is believed to have special powers to influence good and evil spirits – 22 **vinyl** *Schallplatte*

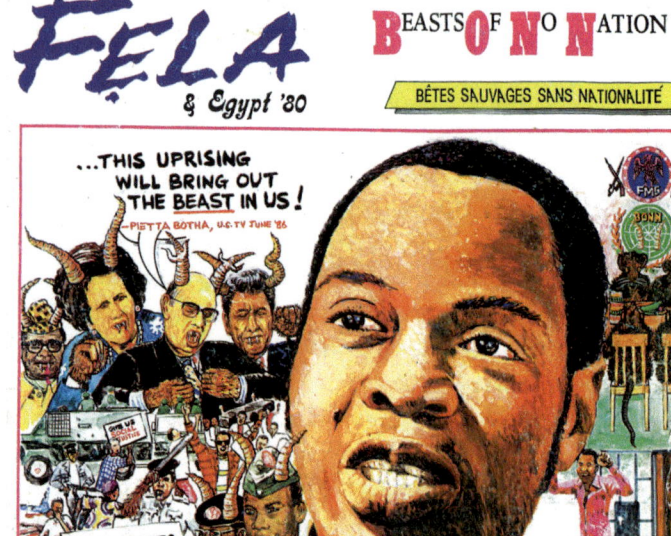

Beasts Of No Nation (B.O.N.N.) was Fela's attack on his jailers for an eighteen-month undeserved incarceration from a trumped-up currency trafficking charge. Smarting from his experience in jail, Fela throws his punches like an enraged prize-fighter. In typical Fela style, *Beasts Of No Nation* made the acronym BONN, which is a disguised reference to the once de facto capital city of West Germany and the days of Adolf Hitler's Nazism.

The music is as powerful as it gets and beneath his knife-edge, cutting sarcasm, Fela's voice rages. It would take a serious sleeve to convey that acid tone. I knew I had to depict the evils of South African apartheid, and the failures and hypocrisy of the United Nations. I made the delegates look like rats, and I portrayed the oppressors with animal's horns and fangs; the slavering vampires of Margaret Thatcher, South Africa's Prime Minister, P.W. Botha, Ronald Reagan and President Mobutu Sese Seko of Zaire cram the frame. The quote used on the top left of the cover art is from a speech by Botha, and among my beasts are Generals Mohammed Buhari and Babatunde Idiagbon, the men responsible for Fela's 1984 jail stint. The images of *Beasts of No Nation* seethe with primal urges – greed, control, vengeance – and the spirit of defiance is embodied in the demonstrators waving a placard with a line from the song, 'Human Rights Is Our Property'. The demonstrators wear Black Power sunglasses and their pink tracksuits pulsate with pastel against the sombre palette of their enemies. Fela's costume is the same exuberant pink, and their gestures are echoed in his triumphant Black Power salute, as he faces them across the frame, while the offending judge cowers at his feet.

---

2 **trumped-up** invented, fake – 3 **to traffic** to illegally buy or sell sth – 11 **hypocrisy** [hɪˈpɑːkrəsi] *Scheinheiligkeit, Heuchelei* – 15 **to cram** to fill – 19 **to seethe** to be crowded with sth – 20 **vengeance** [ˈvendʒəns] desire to harm or take revenge on sb – 24 **sombre** dark

Fela decided to make an incursion into the various untouchable aspects of our society. He took advantage of the sweet and seductive power of those things that are looked upon as taboo and he invited Nigeria to the debate, and I stand with resoluteness behind him to this day.

© Lemi Ghariokwu

---

1 **incursion** *Eindringen*

Text 4: Nollywood Dreams

b*y Jocelyn Bioh (2018)*

Jocelyn Bioh is a Ghanaian-American playwright, writer and actor. Her plays, including the award-winning "School Girls", are often
5 *comedies that address stereotypes of colorism.*

   Her play "Nollywood Dreams" deals with the explosion in the 1990s—a time of economic and political turmoil—of the Nigerian film industry, or Nollywood as it is frequently called. Although these films often told stories of love and/or family issues, they were often rooted in
10 *subtext about the political strife of the country. Back then they were mostly low-budget productions that were released directly onto video.*

   Today, Nollywood is the second largest film industry in the world after Bollywood. Annual revenue is rumoured to be around \$3 billion and over 2,000 films are produced each year.

15 *The extract we have included here opens with Adenikeh, Nigeria's answer to Oprah Winfrey interviewing Gbenga Ezie, Nigeria's hottest director, who has decided to host an open casting for the female lead in his new film. We also meet two of the women hoping to make an impression and win the role, Fayola Ogunleye, a former child star who*
20 *has recently returned from pursuing a movie career in the US, and Ayamma Okafor, a travel agent with big dreams of a better life as an actress.*

Adenikeh Episode Clip—#1

Adenikeh is in the midst of an interview with Gbenga Ezie.
The Adenikeh theme song fades out.

ADENIKEH. And welcome back to Adenikeh. Today, as I bring love
into your home, I bring in tow the hottest Nollywood movie
director, Gbenga Ezie.

Light claps from the audience.

GBENGA. Thank you Adenikeh. It is always wonderful to be on
your show.

ADENIKEH. Now before the break, we were talking about your
time in America.

GBENGA. Yes, I spent a couple of years in New York before moving
to Los Angeles and working in Hollywood for a while.

ADENIKEH. And tell me, was your time in Hollywood the
inspiration to bring a new kind of business model to Nigeria?

GBENGA. Yes, it is important to me to make Nollywood as
competitive a market as Hollywood is. Nigerian movies can be just
as mainstream as any American film. We are a thriving country with
a lot of talent that needs to be showcased as well. So yes, I think it
is important we implement the audition process, script development,
media tours, and create funding for big budget studio films.

ADENIKEH. Yes, and I'm sure you met quite a few characters at
your time at NYU. New York University, for those of you who don't
know, is one of the most prestigious schools in America and Gbenga
received a full scholarship into the Film program.

---

18 thriving successful, fortunate – **21 funding** supply of money

GBENGA. Uh …yes. Yes, I did. And I met all sorts of amazing people who helped me further my career along.

ADENIKEH. In fact, it was at NYU that you began to write the initial script for *The Comfort Zone*, yes?

5 GBENGA. Yes, that is true. I wrote the script and everyone in the industry was fighting for it. Martin Scorsese, Steven Spielberg—all of them wanted my movie and finally in my last studio meeting, I said, "You know what Mr. Coppola, I think I am going to take my script back to my homeland."

10 ADENIKEH. And we are so glad that you did. Aren't we all anxiously awaiting to see Wale Owusu on screen again, ladies?

The audience cheers, claps, and whistles.

So about *The Comfort Zone*, as I understand, it is about a man struggling to find out where his true love lies: with his wife in

15 America or his Nigerian love, Comfort.

GBENGA. Yes. It is an intriguing story of a very complicated love triangle.

ADENIKEH. And what was the inspiration behind the tortured heart of this man? Is there any truth to the rumors that this may

20 just, in fact, be based on your own life?

The audience "ooh"s and "ahh"s with intrigue.

GBENGA. I did meet a man when I was in the States whose story was similar to this, but I assure you, it has nothing to do with me.

ADENIKEH. I see ... And I mean, it's not like you have been married

25 before … Have you?!

---

6 **Martin Scorsese** (*1942), **Steven Spielberg** (*1946) well-known, successful American filmmakers – 8 **Francis Ford Coppola (*1939)** American filmmaker – 10 **anxious** [ˈæŋ(k)ʃəs] *here*: very keen, eager – 16 **intriguing** very interesting, fascinating

GBENGA. Adenikeh, come now. If I was married, surely I would not hide it.

ADENIKEH. Yes, I know. It is a trait that many people admire about you—your honesty. But, the issue you are addressing in this movie is poignant—sham marriages are plaguing many of our Nigerian men as are the recent surge of these internet scams. All of these things are truly bringing shame to our people. Don't you agree?

GBENGA. Umm, yes, I do. And sadly, I have to say… I too was tempted to go down that road.

The audience gasps in shock.

ADENIKEH. *(Dramatic…shocked.)* Were you?!
GBENGA. *Yes, but thankfully, I* uh …chose *differently.*

The audience is relieved.

ADENIKEH. (Re: relief sounds.) So am I!
GBENGA. I want to show the world, through my films, that we are a nation of innovators and creatives. We are more than the poverty-stricken criminals we are perceived to be. And film is a powerful way to convey that.

ADENIKEH. Wow! Look at you—trying to change the world!
GBENGA. I hope so.
ADENIKEH. But for now, you are trying to change the life of one very lucky young actress with the announcement of your *Comfort Zone* Open Casting Call!

GBENGA. That's right. I want to see any and all talent that we have here in Nigeria. So if you are eighteen years and older and have an interest in being an actress, regardless of your experience, please

---

5 **poignant** ['pɔɪnjənt] causing sadness – 5 **sham** fake – 6 **surge** sudden increase

head down to my Nollywood Dreams Movie Studio and sign up to audition for the role of Comfort.

The audience cheers loudly.

ADENIKEH. Well, it is time for us to take a short break, but we will be back with our in-depth interview with Gbenga Ezie. Do not change from this program.

The audience claps as the Adenikeh theme song plays out. A camera operator is heard saying, "And cut. Two minutes until we're back." Gbenga and Adenikeh relax a bit, sip water, etc.

So this *Comfort Zone* movie sounds very exciting, eh?
GBENGA. Oh yes. I'm hoping it will do very well.
ADENIKEH. Me too… You know I used to do a bit of acting myself.
GBENGA. Oh yeah?
ADENIKEH. I mean, it's been a long time, but I'm sure it's like riding a bike you know?
GBENGA. Exactly. Talent is talent.
ADENIKEH. Yeah… and you know… That *Color Purple* movie did wonders for Oprah and her show, so you know, just think of sister Adenikeh when you're writing your next big film, eh?
GBENGA. *(Nervous la*ughter *)* Oh, sure. Of course.

Offstage a camera man is heard: "And we're back in 5. 4. 3. 2…" The Adenikeh theme music plays as the stage transitions into:

---

18 **The Color Purple** (1985) movie based on the 1982 prize-winning book of the same name written by Alice Walker that describes the problems African American women faced in the early 20th century (including domestic violence, racism, sexism, poverty)

Scene 2: Okafor Travel Agency Office

Dede and Ayamma are at their desks. Dede sits with her feet
propped up, sipping tea, eating a snack of some sort, and
reading a magazine. Ayamma is going over her lines
silently—but full of expression. The phone rings for a long
while before Dede begrudgingly picks it up.

DEDE. *(Into phone.)* Thank you for calling Okafor Travels. This is
Dede. How may I help you?

Listens.

Ah yes, just one moment. *(To Ayamma.)* It's for you.
AYAMMA. Who is it?
DEDE. I don't know. Someone who wants to book a flight.
AYAMMA. And why can't you handle it?
DEDE. You don't see that I am doing some important reading here?

Ayamma sucks teeth... picks up call.

AYAMMA. Thank you for holding. This is Ayamma, how may I help
you?

Listens.

Eh, no mam. We do not offer safari packages.

Listens.

Eh, the Serengeti is not in Nigeria... No... No... No wrong part of
Africa. Sorry.

---

6 **begrudgingly** reluctantly, not really wanting to

Sucks teeth as she hangs up.

Stupid Europeans.
DEDE. Africa is a country to them, you know that.
AYAMMA. Well I cannot be bothered with their foolishness today.
I've only got one hour left to perfect this audition.
DEDE. "This audition."
DEDE. Yes, yes, yes, we know. I swear, I cannot wait until it is over because I'm so sick of hearing about it.
AYAMMA. Pardon?
DEDE. Ah, Ayamma, but it's all you've been talking about. Me, I cannot even sleep without dreaming about your lines. *(Mocking.)* "Oh James, you have betrayed me. You've hurt me, Oh, oh, oh!"
AYAMMA. I can see the jealousy written all over your face.
DEDE. Oh please. My only goal right now is to get to Wale. Oh, if you get this movie, you have no idea! Me, I will be on set every day and it will only be a matter of time before Wale takes one look at me and he will collapse. 'Cause his body will not be able to withstand the powerful chemistry we will have. I'm telling you!

Dede continues to read. Ayamma has, just a bit,
"Gone Nollywood" already.

AYAMMA. Dede please! If I—WHEN I get this movie, you won't be able to just hang around. The movie set is a sacred space where very powerful art is being created. You know, I started reading *Acting in Film* and Michael Caine says that true acting—
DEDE. *(Reading.)* Hey… hey did you see this?
AYAMMA. Dede, I don't care about that silly village gossip.
DEDE. Okay, so it's just gossip that Mr. Ezie is considering another girl for the role of Comfort.

---

22 **sacred** *hochheilig*

AYAMMA. What?!

DEDE. *(Reading out loud.)* "Anticipation is building as Gbenga Ezie compiles his list of actors for his new film *The Comfort Zone*. Word has been spreading rapidly that Mr. Ezie is strongly considering former child star turned Nollywood darling Fayola Ogunleye for the lead role of Comfort. Commonly regarded as the 'Nigerian Halle Berry with Tina Turner legs,' her casting would mark the second time Fayola and Wale would work together. Some Olofofo birds in the know claim that last year on the set of *Corporate Office*, Wale and Fayola were alleged to always 'be around each other'. We guess we will have to wait and see if Mr. Ezie will help spark that fire again."

AYAMMA. First above all, she looks nothing like Halle Berry.

DEDE. That is true. I would say more like a close relative… But the "Tina Turner legs"? Dead on.

AYAMMA. Ah! But that is not right. How could he say that he wants fresh faces, but would "strongly consider" her?

DEDE. *(Sarcasm… And eating.)* Oh, but I thought you don't care about silly village gossip?

AYAMMA. I don't!… So what if he is letting Fayola audition? Good for her. I mean, honestly, who is she?

DEDE. Yes, I know it. She just comes from a wealthy family… Men are always going crazy over her… She has already been in several films… AND she knows Wale according to what the Olofofo birds are saying… but hey, you never know. Maybe, he'll skip over her and give you—a modest, homely, village girl—a chance.

Ayamma stares a hole into Dede's head.

You want me to put a curse on her?

---

3 **to compile** to put together, to gather – 8 **olofofo** (*Yoruba*) gossip – 28 **to put a curse on sb** *jdn verfluchen*

AYAMMA. Dede, you know your curses never work.
DEDE. Maybe this will be the one.

The phone rings.

AYAMMA. Whatever. I'm leaving.
DEDE. Where are you going?
AYAMMA. I need to handle some business before I go downtown.

Ayamma begins to hurriedly gather her things.

DEDE. Oh, getting a new, hot outfit at the market? You are nervous now, eh?
AYAMMA. No.

Ayamma continues to collect her things. The phone continues to ring.

DEDE. Eh-eh! But who is going to answer these phone lines?
AYAMMA. Dede, please. Why don't you try doing some work for a change?
DEDE. I do plenty of work around here… And anyway, you are supposed to be handling the business. You know I don't know how to work the computers.
AYAMMA. *(Sighs.)* Can you just do me this one favor? Please? Sista?
DEDE. *(Sucks teeth.)* Fine. But bring me a large pack of ginger cookies while you are at the market.
AYAMMA. *(Quickly.)* Ah, you do not need any more cookies.
DEDE. You say what?
AYAMMA. Nothing. Fine. I've got to go. Wish me luck!

---

20 ginger *Ingwer*

Ayamma rushes out. The phone continues to ring.

DEDE. *(Finally answering.)* Thank you for calling Okafor Travels. This is Dede. How may I help you?

Listens.

⁵ Ehh! Mary! How are you? Oh, fine-fine.

The other phone line begins to ring. Dede ignores it.

Yes, I have time to talk. What's happening with you?

Listens.

That woman came into your salon again?! Is she still wearing that
¹⁰ blonde wig? Who does she think she's fooling? *(Laughs.)* It does look like a coconut tree! Oh Mary you are too much, oh!

Lights shift.

---

10 wig covering for the head made of hair

ADENIKEH EPISODE CLIP—#2

Adenikeh is in the midst of an interview with Fayola Ogunleye.

ADENIKEH. And we're back with our candid interview with former child star turned Nollywood "It" girl Fayola Ogunleye.

Applause from the audience.

FAYOLA. Thank you so much Adenikeh.
ADENIKEH. Fayola, in the press you are commonly referred to as the "Nigerian Halle Berry—"
FAYOLA. "With Tina Turner legs."
ADENIKEH. Uh, yes. How do you feel about being the apple of men's affections and the envy of all women?
FAYOLA. Well, I don't know if I am all of that. Honestly, I am just happy to still be working in this business for nearly twenty years.
ADENIKEH. Yes, many of us remember you as the lovable younger sister Chioma in the hit television series *Family Comes First*.
FAYOLA. That was a wonderful time in my life.
ADENIKEH. You were once the "go to" actress for many popular projects, so, many of us were surprised when you decided to leave Nigeria and pursue a career in America some years ago. What was the meaning of this?
FAYOLA. Honestly… I was in love.

Light "Awww"s from the audience.

My boyfriend at the time had an opportunity to go to America and asked me to come with him.

---

3 **candid** honest, open

ADENIKEH. And your love for him did not allow you to say no?

FAYOLA. He promised me the world and well, I guess you can say I'm a bit of a romantic because I believed him.

ADENIKEH. But he did not give you the world, did he?

FAYOLA. No. Things got... a bit... complicated.

ADENIKEH. Mmm. I understand. And since we are speaking candidly, it is common knowledge that the last few films that you have starred in have not fared well. Do you believe that your time away from the spotlight here in Nigeria is the cause of you losing your fan base?

FAYOLA. It is the nature of this business, Adenikeh. Some movies do well and others don't. But I am working on some new, exciting projects now and I have a feeling that things will go my way. Trust me, the fans will be very excited.

ADENIKEH. Yes, we have heard some rumblings of you perhaps reuniting on screen with the handsome Wale Owusu.

The audience hoots and whistles at the thought of Wale Owusu.

FAYOLA. *(Over the cheering.)* Oh, so you all like to see that, eh?!

ADENIKEH. And as for this mystery gentleman—the man who broke your heart—have you forgiven him for the wishes he did not fulfill?

FAYOLA. Of course... I was taught to forgive others for their mistakes. None of us are perfect.

ADENIKEH. Well, I do not know. I would say that if I had legs like yours, I would feel pretty close to perfect.

The audience claps and cheers.

FAYOLA. *(Crossing her legs; trying to be coy.)* Oh Adenikeh, you are too much, oh.

ADENIKEH. *(To camera.)* Okay, well we must take a short break here. Do not turn off your television sets. More with Fayola Ogunleye after these messages.

> *The audience claps and cheers as the Adenikeh theme song plays out.*

Scene 3: Ezie's Nollywood Dreams Studios

> *Gbenga and Fayola exit a studio room and spill into the lobby, laughing and carrying on like old friends.*

GBENGA. Eh, Fayola. I'm so glad that you came in to read for me… I have been waiting for us to be able to work together again.

FAYOLA. Really?

GBENGA. Yes. I kept thinking how perfect you would be for this movie.

FAYOLA. Well, if I'm so perfect, why have auditions then?

GBENGA. Come now, you know from our time in America, nothing gets people more excited than an open call. You see how good the publicity has been already and we have not even started shooting. I want to ensure this movie will be a hit.

FAYOLA. Eh! Look at you—"publicity"… Using the "Media"… Bringing Hollywood to Nollywood, eh?

GBENGA. Well, my time in Los Angeles taught me a lot.

FAYOLA. I see that. And you've written a great script. Comfort is an amazing role.

GBENGA. And I think you would be perfect in it.

---

1 **coy** pretending to be shy

FAYOLA. Thank you… I was worried that maybe you were considering me for Rose. Not that it's not a great part, but come on—I'm no supporting actress.

GBENGA. Of course. If anyone knows that, it is me…

5   *They both laugh a bit. Beat.*

You know, I was surprised to learn you were back in Nigeria for good. I heard from some people that you were splitting your time between here and New York?

FAYOLA. I was… for a while. I got connected to a talent agent there.
10   So I was going on auditions and the sort. But it was hard, oh. Always going in for some foolish thing… Slaves… House workers.

GBENGA. Yes, these parts they have for Black Americans.

FAYOLA. But was it English or what? I would be reading the paper, *(Really bad slave dialect accent.)* "I's a gonna be gwan down to de
15   swamp an' pick me some cott'in"… What is this?

GBENGA. Yes, yes. It's some sort of old dialect. I don't understand it myself.

FAYOLA. *(Sucks teeth.)* It was too much. So a year ago, I decided to come back home for good. Work on the films that were true to me.
20   To our people, you know? Like yours.

GBENGA. Ah yes, I definitely understand.

FAYOLA. I, uh, hear that you have hired Wale to play the role of James.

GBENGA. Yes, that's correct.

25   FAYOLA. He seems nice. We worked together briefly once, but not in a romantic role.

GBENGA. Yeah, he is a really good guy. I think you two would have great chemistry.

---

14 **gwan** going (mainly Caribbean dialect)

FAYOLA. Oh really?

GBENGA. But not too much, oh! Save some for others.

Beat.

FAYOLA. It's nice to see things are going well for you and your, eh, computer business. It really seems to be taking off.

GBENGA. Oh yes, business is great. You know, this internet thing is very fast growing. My brothers and I are about to open up another center in a few months.

FAYOLA. Good for you. I always said that all of you Ezie men are very ambitious... I see you haven't stopped chasing the American dream.

GBENGA. I cannot argue with you on that one.

FAYOLA. Hmm... That may be the only thing you cannot argue with me about.

GBENGA. Really Fayola?

FAYOLA. What? I did not say anything.

GBENGA. I have learned with you women, you do not need to say words to speak loudly.

FAYOLA. "You women" eh? ...Oh, so I guess that eye of yours still likes to wander about.

GBENGA. Ah, Fayola, what is this, eh? I thought we decided to leave all of that in the past.

FAYOLA. You're right, you're right. I'm sorry I even brought it up. It's been four years and I'm over it and you are over it, so let's just, you know... keep it business only.

GBENGA. I agree... Business only.

© Jocelyn Bioh

Make notes here on what this section has contributed to
your bigger picture of "Voices of Africa – Nigeria"

2 The bloody road to democracy

Introduction

The road to democracy in Nigeria has not been a smooth one. As one of the main centres of the transatlantic slave trade in the 18th and 19th centuries, more than 3.5 million slaves were shipped from Nigeria to the Americas, where they were forced to work on cotton and tobacco plantations. They lost all individual rights as human beings and were little more than the property of their owners.

In 1900 the British Empire created the Southern Nigerian Protectorate and the Northern Nigerian Protectorate which were united in 1914 as the Colony and Protectorate of Nigeria. Indigenous Nigerians governed their country via "indirect rule" for more than three generations. Christian Missionaries established Western educational institutions, influencing the mélange of indigenous peoples with modern science, European technology, education, medicine and Christian belief.

After Nigeria's independence in 1960 a long period of political and social instability followed: from the beginning there was ethnic and religious tension between the north and the south. The fight for access to the oil-rich regions of the country, economic injustices and large-scale massacres resulted in a bloody civil war, the Biafran War.

The texts in this section highlight some of the more recent but no less shocking and bloody chapters in Nigeria's history since independence.

Tasks

1. Summarize Nigeria's present-day internal security challenges and draw connections to its history as well as its social development.

2. In smaller groups: discuss possible ways to support a country to find its own strong, stable identity and to deal with some of the problems mentioned in the texts.

Text 1: There Was a Country

by Chinua Achebe (2012)

Chinua Achebe is considered one of the founding fathers of modern African literature and one of the most passionate chroniclers of Nigeria's troubled history. A novelist, poet and essayist, Achebe is best known for his first novel, "Things Fall Apart", published in 1958. It has sold over 10m copies around the world and has been published in 50 languages. As Nelson Mandela once said, Achebe "brought Africa to the rest of the world".

His last work published before his death in March 2013 is the memoir "There was a country", an account of the Nigerian civil war of 1967 to 1970. In it Achebe outlines the events that led to the civil war, the course it ran and the aftermath. But it is also a deeply personal account of how he and his family survived the bloody conflict.

We have four extracts from the memoir. The first recounts the events immediately after the first military coup of January 15th 1966, sixteen months before the civil war started. The second briefly describes life in Biafra and the third the collapse of the Biafran Republic after only thirty months. In the final extract Achebe reflects upon the state of unified Nigeria in the post-war period and the challenges it faced then and still faces to this day.

Extract 1: The Dark Days

On January 16, 1966 the day after the Nzeogwu coup, my wife, Christie, took our first child, Chinelo, to the movies to catch the matinee. Chinelo was full of energy—always running all over the
5 place. My wife's doctor, Dr. Okoronkwo Ogan, who became our daughter's godfather, called her "quicksilver." On their way home, my wife decided to drop by and see me in the office, so that our daughter could tell me all about the movie they had watched. I believe it was the Disney classic *Dumbo*, about the flying elephant.
10 As they approached the Nigerian Broadcasting Corporation they saw the soldiers around but did not know what was happening. They were not scared, even though they found the commotion a bit peculiar.

As they walked to my office someone yelled at my wife: "Where
15 are you going? Don't you know what is happening?" So she walked more briskly, because she wanted to find out whether I was alive. A soldier stopped them and asked them to leave. They returned home and tuned into the radio station to find out what was going on.

People were standing on the streets in small groups, listening to
20 the radios of street newspaper vendors. There had been a coup, the radio announcers said, at which point there was an initial period of spontaneous, overt jubilation. The story of the coup and how it happened started leaking out, first from the military barracks and then from the international media. There was a great deal of anxiety
25 among the general populace. Everyone wanted to find out exactly what had happened in Kaduna, Lagos, Ibadan, and elsewhere the night before, though apparently not much action had been seen in

---

2 **Nzeogwu coup** military coup led by C.K. Nzeogwu on 15 January 1966. 22 people were killed including the Nigerian Prime Minister and his family – 4 **matinee** movie shown at the cinema in the afternoon – 12 **commotion** sudden state of noise and confusion – 20 **vendor** a person or company that sells sth – 25 **populace** population

Enugu, the capital of the Eastern Region. The initial vacuum of information was filled with gossip, innuendo, and fabricated accounts that magnified the confusion throughout the country. A second story got around that the military coup, which at first had been so well received, was in fact a sinister plot by the ambitious Igbo of the East to seize control of Nigeria.

In a country in which tribalism was endemic, the rumor of an "Igbo coup" began to find acceptance. Before long many people were persuaded that their spontaneous jubilation in January had been a mistake. A Nigerian poet who had dedicated a new book "to the heroes of January 1966" had second thoughts after the countercoup of July, and he sent a frantic cable to his publishers to remove the dedication.

Those who knew Nigeria were not very surprised, because part of the way to respond to confusion in Nigeria is to blame those from the other ethnic group or the other side of the country. One found some ethnic or religious element supporting whatever one was trying to make sense of. This angle grew stronger and stronger as the days passed, mainly because the state of confusion was not really dispelled satisfactorily by the authorities.

The weeks following the coup saw Easterners attacked both randomly and in an organized fashion. There seemed to be a lust for revenge, which meant an excuse for Nigerians to take out their resentment on the Igbo who led the nation in virtually every sector—politics, education, commerce, and the arts. This group, the Igbo, that gave the colonizing British so many headaches and then literally drove them out of Nigeria was now an open target, scapegoats for the failings and grievances of colonial and post-independence Nigeria.

---

2 **innuendo** hint or suggestion about sb that may or may not be true – 7 **endemic** natural, characteristic – 12 **frantic** desperate – 12 **cable** *Telegramm* – 28 **scapegoat** *Sündenbock* – 28 **grievance** [ˈgriːvəns] complaint, resentment

It was a desperate time. Soldiers were being used by elements in power to commit a number of crimes against Igbo, Nigerian citizens. Military officers were rounding people up and summarily executing them, particularly in the North, we were told by victims fleeing the pogroms. There was a story of hoodlums looking to hunt down and kill Dr. Okechukwu Ikejiani, who was the chairman of the Nigerian Coal Corporation. Dr. Ikejiani escaped the grasp of these thugs by dressing up as a woman and crossing the Nigeria border to Dahomey (today's Republic of Benin)!

In Lagos, where we lived, soldiers were also used in targeted raids of certain people's homes, including our own. It happened that my wife and I had moved recently from Milverton Street to Turnbull Road, after my promotion to director of external broadcasting. Fortunately for us the soldiers went to Milverton Street, to our old house, to search for me.

Some may wonder why soldiers would be after me so fervently. As I mentioned, it happened that I had just written *A Man of the People*, which forecast a military coup that overthrows a corrupt civilian government. Clearly a case of fact imitating fiction and nothing else, but some military leaders believed that I must have had something to do with the coup and wanted to bring me in for questioning.

Eventually my family and I left our Turnbull Road house, a painful decision. We had moved into it after we were married. It was located in Ikoyi; a nice section of town, overlooking the lagoon. I remember receiving important visitors in our home, such as the great African American poet Langston Hughes, who stopped by during one of his famous African tours. I have a favorite picture of the two of us from that period, standing near a palm tree on the lawn of that lovely residence.

---

5 **pogrom** organized massacre, mass killing – 5 **hoodlum** gangster, criminal – 27 **Langston Hughes** (1901–1967) American poet, social activist, novelist and playwright

We found refuge in an old friend's house—Frank Cawson, the British Council representative in Lagos, whose intervention literally saved our lives. He housed us for a number of days. Mr. Cawson had been the British Council representative in Accra, Ghana, and had invited me to give a lecture there before he came to Lagos. I delivered a lecture, entitled, "The African Writer and the English Language." So when Mr. Cawson was transferred to Nigeria, he was already known to me.

He was monitoring local and international radio and newspapers to get a sense of what was happening. He took a number of precautionary steps to enhance our safety. First he took his car out of the garage and put our own there instead, so that no one would see it. It was a very tense, anxiety-plagued period for my wife and me and our two children, Chinelo, who was five years old, and Ike, who was two. Making matters worse was the fact that Frank Cawson was quite ill—I think with malaria.

For about a week, lying hidden in Mr. Cawson's house in Lagos, I still simply thought that things had temporarily gotten out of hand, and that everything would soon be all right. Then, suddenly, I discovered that I had been operating on a false and perhaps naïve basis all along. The soldiers located us after we had been hiding about a week. It became clear to me that I had to send my family away.

As many of us packed our belongings to return east some of the people we had lived with for years, some for decades, jeered and said, "Let them {Igbo} go; food will be cheaper in Lagos." That kind of experience is very powerful. It is something I could not possibly forget. I realized suddenly that I had not been living in my home; I had been living in a strange place. There were more and more reports of massacres, and not only in the North, but also in the West

---

11 **precautionary** *vorbeugend, vorsorglich* – 25 **to jeer** to laugh and shout insults at sb

and in Lagos. People were hounded out of their homes, as we were
in Lagos, and returned to the East. We expected to hear something
from the intellectuals, from our friends. Rather, what we heard was,
"Oh, they had it coming to them," or words to that effect. There were
many others from other parts of Nigeria who did not jeer but
suffered with us at this sudden discovery that a section of the large,
diverse Nigerian family was not welcome in this new country.

A lot of this hot-blooded anger was fanned by British intellectuals
and some radical Northern elements in places like Ahmadu Bello
University. They were aided by a few in the expatriate population
from outside Nigeria, who easily influenced the mostly self-satisfied
and docile Northern leadership to activate a weapon that has been
used repeatedly in Nigeria's short history—a fringe element known
as "area boys" or the "rent-a-crowd types"—to attack Igbo in an
orgy of blood.

As we reached the brink of full-blown war it became clear to me
that the chaos enveloping all of us in Nigeria was due to the
incompetence of the Nigerian ruling class. They clearly bad a poor
grasp of history and found it difficult to appreciate and grapple with
Nigeria's ethnic and political complexity. This clique, stunted by
ineptitude, distracted by power games and the pursuit of material
comforts, was unwilling, if not incapable, of saving our fledgling
new nation.

---

8 **to fan** *here*: to spread – 12 **docile** easily controlled – 19 **to grapple with sth** to try to
understand sth – 21 **ineptitude** lack of skill or ability – 22 **fledgling** young

Extract 2: Life in Biafra

The Nigeria-Biafra conflict created a humanitarian emergency of epic proportions. Millions of civilians—grandparents, mothers, fathers, children, and soldiers alike—flooded the main highway arteries between towns and villages fleeing the chaos and conflict. They traveled by foot, by truck, by car, barefoot, with slippers, in wheelbarrows, many in wornout shoes. Some had walked so long their soles were blistered and bleeding. As hunger and thirst grew, so did despair, confusion, and desperation. Most were heading in whatever direction the other was headed, propelled by the latest rumors of food and shelter spreading through the multitude like a virus. Refugees were on the move in no specific direction, anywhere, just away from the fighting. As they fled the war zones they became targets of the Nigerian air force. The refugees learned to travel nights and hide in the forests by day.

The international relief agencies started responding to the growing humanitarian challenge quite early in the conflict by establishing food distribution centers and refugee camps. There were many Biafran refugee camps dotting the landscape, from Enugu in the north to Owerri in the south, during the thirty-month conflict. Many held between a few hundred and a few thousand people. At the height of the war there were well over three thousand such centers and camps, a great number but woefully inadequate to the actual need.

These camps were often hastily constructed tent villages set up beside bombed-out churches, in football or sports arenas, or in open fields in the forest. They uniformly lacked electricity, running water, or other comforts. Occasionally, the more established camps had sturdier shelters on the premises of abandoned schools or

---

23 **woefully** badly – 29 **to abandon** to leave, evacuate

colleges, or built near freshwater streams or little rivers. Those were few and far between. Most had rows of mud huts and palm raffia roofs built hastily by the inhabitants themselves. They were occasionally fenced in by the international agencies, which placed guards on the camp perimeter to monitor movement in and out of the area. The relief agencies often hoisted their flags to indicate to the Nigerian officers that they were in neutral zones that should be protected from assault. That did not always keep the Nigerian troops from raiding these "safe havens," or even from bombing them.

Life in the camps varied in quality. Some of the better organized camps provided water, shelter, food, basic health care—mainly vaccinations for children against the most prevalent diseases, and treatment of common bacterial infections—and education. Other camps could only be described as deplorable, epidemic-ridden graveyards. In these camps the combination of poor sanitation, high population density, and shortages of supplies created a bitter cocktail of despair, giving rise to social pathologies and psychological traumas of all kinds—violence, extortion, and physical and sexual abuse.

My siblings and their families returned to my father's house in Ogidi from various parts of the country. My family did too: Christie and my children at the time, Chinelo and Ike, left Port Harcourt for my family's ancestral home.

My village is about six miles from Onitsha, the commercial hub of Eastern Nigeria and the location of the largest market in West Africa. Onitsha is also where the famous Niger Bridge is located, and so it serves as the entry point for all travelers entering the East

---

5 **perimeter** outer edge or border of an area – 12 **vaccination** *Impfung* – 16 **population density** *Bevölkerungsdichte*

from points west. The close proximity of Ogidi to Onitsha meant that we were in the eye of the storm, as it were, right at the border of the conflict. We were so close to the war zone we could hear the sounds of war—heavy artillery fire, bombs, and machine-gun fights.

By the time I left Lagos to join my family in Ogidi, there were rumors that the Nigerian army was not that far behind. Casting my mind back, I am surprised at how little pandemonium there was during the early stages of the conflict. Families casually began to move deeper into the countryside to prepare for the inevitability of war.

Food was short, meat was very short, and drugs were short. Thousands—no, millions by then—had been uprooted from their homes and brought into safer areas, but where they really had no relatives, no property; many of them lived in school buildings and camps. The Committee for Biafran Refugees, understandably overwhelmed, did what it could. I found it really quite amazing how much people were ready to give.

Beyond the understandable trepidation associated with a looming war, one found a new spirit among the people, a spirit one did not know existed, a determination, in fact. The spirit was that of a people ready to put in their best and fight for their freedom. Biafran churches made links to the persecution of the early Christians, others on radio to the Inquisition and the persecution of the Jewish people. The prevalent mantra of the time was "*Ojukwu nye anyi egbe ka anyi nuo agha*"—"Ojukwu give us guns to fight a war." It was an energetic, infectious duty song, one sung to a well-known melody and used effectively to recruit young men into the

---

7 **pandemonium** chaos – 18 **trepidation** fear – 22 **persecution** unfair or cruel treatment because of race, religion etc. – 24 **mantra** often repeated word, formula, phrase – 24 **Ojukwu** C. Odumegwu Ojukwu (1933–2011) Nigerian military officer and politician, leader of the Republic of Biafra from 1967 to 1970

People's Army (the army of the Republic of Biafra). But in the early Stages of the war, when the Biafran army grew quite rapidly, sadly Ojukwu had no guns to give to those brave souls.

But the most vital feeling Biafrans had at that time was that they were finally in a safe place ... at home. This was the first and most important thing, and one could see this sense of exhilaration in the effort that the people were putting into the war. Young girls, for example, had taken over the job of controlling traffic. They were really doing it by themselves—no one asked them to. That this kind of spirit existed made us feel tremendously hopeful. Clearly something had happened to the psyche of an entire people to bring this about.

Richard West, a British journalist, was so captivated by the meticulous nature with which Biafrans conducted the affairs of state that he wrote a widely cited article in which he larnented: "Biafra is more than a human tragedy. Its defeat, I believe, would mark the end of African independence. Biafra was the first place I had been to in Africa where the Africans themselves were truly in charge."

---

14 **meticulous** very careful, precise

Extract 3: 1970 and The Fall

[…]

In the end, Biafra collapsed. We simply had to turn around and find a way to keep those people still there alive. It was a desperate
5 situation, with so many children in need, kwashiorkor rampant, and thousands perishing every week. The notoriously incompetent Nigerian government was not responding to those in need quickly enough. With illadvised bravado Gowon was busy banning relief agencies that had helped Biafra. It was in this environment of
10 desperation that some people said, Let's go into the forest and continue the struggle. That would have been suicidal, and I don't think anybody should commit suicide.

We had spent nearly three years fighting, fighting for a cause, fighting to the finish … for freedom. But all that had collapsed, and
15 Biafra with it. A very bitter experience had led to it in the first place. And the big powers prolonged it.

You see we, the little people of the world, are ever expendable. The big powers can play their games even if millions perish in the process. And perish they did. In the end millions (some state upward
20 of three million, mostly children) had died, mainly from starvation due to the federal government of Nigeria's blockade policies.

General Gowon made a national broadcast on the eve of the official surrender to announce the end of the thirty-month war that he said had claimed over one hundred thousand military service
25 men and women and over three million Biafrans. His "no victor, no

---

5 **kwashiorkor** [ˌkwɒʃiˈɔːkɔː] severe form of malnutrition due to a long period without food – 5 **rampant** widespread, spreading quickly – 6 **to perish** to die – 8 **bravado** very bold confidence – 8 **Gowon** Yakubu Gowon (*1934) head of state of Nigeria from 1966–1975. He ruled during the Biafran War, during which approximately 3 million people died. –
25 **"no victor, no vanquished"** *kein Sieger, keine Besiegten*

vanquished" speech as it has come to be known, strove to strike a conciliatory tone, calling for the full reintegration of Igbo into the fabric of Nigerian life. There was great celebration throughout Nigeria and Biafra at the news of the end of the hostilities.

A day later, on January 15, 1970, the Biafran delegation, which was led by Major General Philip Effiong and included Sir Louis Mbanefo, M. T. Mbu, Colonel David Ogunewe, and other Biafran military officers, formally surrendered at Dodan Barracks to the troops of the Federal Republic of Nigeria. Among the Nigerian delegation were: General Yakubu Gowon; the deputy chairman of the Supreme Military Council, Obafemi Awolowo; leaders of the various branches of the armed forces, including Brigadier Hassan Katsina, chief of staff; H. E. A. Ejueyitchie, the secretary to the federal military government; Anthony Enahoro, the commissioner for information; Taslim Elias, the attorney general; and the twelve military governors of the federation.

At the end of the thirty-month war Biafra was a vast smoldering rubble. The head count at the end of the war was perhaps three million dead, which was approximately 20 percent of the entire population. This high proportion was mostly children. The cost in human lives made it one of the bloodiest civil wars in human history.

The sequelae of wars often begin with an armistice. The suffering and humanitarian disaster left in the wake of war's destruction goes on long after the weapons are silenced—for months and years. Entire towns and villages, schools and farms in Biafra were destroyed. Roads and the rural areas were littered with landmines that continued to maim and kill unsuspecting pedestrians well after

---

17 **to smolder** to burn without flames – 18 **rubble** pieces of broken material, ruins –
23 **sequelae** [sɪˈkwiːleɪ] *(pl)* consequences, aftereffects – 23 **armistice** *Waffenstillstand* –
27 **be littered with sth** be filled with

the hostilities ended. Many people had lost all that they owned. Loved ones in the thousands were reported missing by families. There were stories of scores of suicides. This was not just a case of Ani, or the land and its protector, the land goddess, "bleeding," as my people would describe catastrophic events of this nature. It was worse: a case of Ani nearly "exsanguinating to death."

My generation had great expectations for our young nation. After the war everything we had known before about Nigeria, all the optimism, had to be rethought. The worst had happened, and we were now forced into reorganizing our thinking, expectations, and hopes. We (the former Biafrans) had to carry on in spite of the great disaster that was military defeat and learn very quickly to live with such a loss. We would have to adjust to the realities and consequences of a Nigeria that did not appeal to us any longer. Nigeria had not succeeded in crushing the spirit of the Igbo people, but it had left us indigent, stripped bare, and stranded in the wilderness.

---

6 **to exsanguinate** to lose all blood – 16 **indigent** very poor

Extract 4: Nigeria's Painful Transitions: A Reappraisal

The post Nigeria-Biafra civil war era saw a "unified" Nigeria saddled with a greater and more insidious reality. We were plagued by a homegrown enemy: the political ineptitude, mediocrity, indiscipline, ethnic bigotry, and corruption of the ruling class. Compounding the situation was the fact that Nigeria was now awash in oil-boom petrodollars, and to make matters even worse, the country's young, affable, military head of state, General Yakubu Gowon, ever so cocksure following his victory, proclaimed to the entire planet that Nigeria had more money than it knew what to do with. A new era of great decadence and decline was born. It continues to this day.

At this point, the intellectuals, particularly the writers, were faced with a conundrum. We could no longer pass off this present problem simply to our complicated past and the cold war raging in the background, however significant these factors were. We could not absolve ourselves from the need to take hold of the events of the day and say, Okay, we have had a difficult past. … From today, this is the program we have; let's look at what we have not done. Of course, putting it this dramatically makes the matter appear simple.

However, it became crystal clear that we needed to fight this new enemy with everything at our disposal. Most important, Nigeria needed to identify the right leader with the right kind of character, education, and background. Someone who would understand what was at stake—where Africa had been, and where it needed to go. For the second time in our short history we had to face the disturbing fact that Nigeria needed to liberate itself anew, this time not from a foreign power but from our own corrupt, inept brothers and sisters!

---

4 **insidious** *heimtükisch, hinterhältig* – 5 **mediocrity** low quality – 6 **bigotry** *here:* discrimination – 8 **petrodollars** *(pl)* money earned by selling oil to other countries – 14 **conundrum** difficult problem – 17 **to absolve** to declare sb not guilty or responsible

After waiting around a while and determining that no messiah was about to come down and save the day, some of us joined the political process. I joined the left-of-center Peoples Redemption Party and was appointed its deputy national president. The goal of being an active participant in Nigerian politics would be to elevate the national discourse to a level that stirred up the pot, if you like, and got Nigerians to begin to ask critical questions about their future, such as: How can the country conduct free and fair elections? How can we elect the right kind of leaders and ensure that they will keep to the tenure that was agreed upon? How do we ensure that our leaders don't double their tenure, or even change it into a dynasty to hand over to their sons?

My sojourn in politics was marked by disappointment, frustration, and the realization that despite the fact that there were a few upright political figures like Mallam Aminu Kano, the vast majority of the characters I encountered in the political circles were there for their own selfish advancement. Having grand ideas was fine, but their execution required a strong leader. And clearly, Nigeria's principal problem was identifying and putting in place that elusive leader.

That road to a remedy of Nigeria's political problems will not come easily. The key, as I see it, lies in the manner in which the leadership of the country is selected. When I refer to leadership I am really talking about leaders at every level of government and sphere of society, from the local government council and governors right up to the presidency. What I am calling for is for Nigeria to develop a version of campaign election and campaign finance reform, so that

---

10 **tenure** period of time sb holds an important job – 13 **sojourn** [ˈsoʊdʒɜːrn] temporary period or status – 15 **Mallam Aminu Kano** (1920–1983) Nigerian politician with reformist ideas, who led a socialist movement in opposition to British rule in the 1940s

the country can transform its political system from the grassroots level right through to the national party structures at the federal level.

Nigerians will have to find a way to do away with the present system of godfatherism—an archaic, corrupt practice in which individuals with lots of money and time to spare (many of them half-baked, poorly educated thugs) sponsor their chosen candidates and push them right through to the desired political position, bribing, threatening, and, on occasion, murdering any opposition in the process. We will have to make sure that the electoral body overseeing elections is run by widely respected and competent officials chosen by a nonpartisan group free of governmental influence or interference. Finally, we have to find a way to open up the political process to every Nigerian citizen. Today we have a system where only those individuals with the means of capital and who can both pay the exorbitant application fee and fund a political campaign can vie for the presidency. It would not surprise any close observer to discover that in this inane system, the same unsavory characters who have destroyed the country and looted the treasury and the nation blind are the ones able to run for the presidency!

The question of choice in selecting a leader in Nigeria is often an academic exercise, due to the election rigging, violence, and intimidation of the general public, particularly by those in power, but also by those with the means—the rich and influential. There is also the unpleasant factor of the violence associated with partisan politics that is often designed to keep balanced, well-educated, fair-minded Nigerians away. So it can be said that the masses—the followership we are concerned about—don't really have a choice of leadership, because there's not a true democratic process.

---

16 **exorbitant** very big, very high – 25 **partisan** biased, strongly supporting a particular person, party or cause and lacking willingness to compromise

It may appear impossible now to rectify, because we've allowed this situation of confusion to go on since our independence. It has been growing steadily worse … and it accelerated particularly under the military, when there was a near total denial of the democratic rights of the people. The general knowledge that a people have, for example, inalienable rights is simply something advanced societies take for granted, because they have fostered stable democracies now for some time. I am asked, "Why don't the people fight back?" Well, once a people have been dispossessed and subjugated by dictatorships for such a long time as in Nigeria's case, the oppressive process also effectively strips away from the minds of the people the knowledge that they have rights. Restoring flawed democratic systems will not make the country a success overnight.

© Chinua Achebe

---

1 **to rectify** to make sth right – 7 **to foster** to promote, to encourage, to support –
9 **to subjugate** to bring under complete control

Text 2: Beasts of No Nation

by Uzodinma Iweala (2005)

Uzodinma Iweala is an American writer and doctor of Nigerian descent. Iweala's final thesis at Harvard University on the subject of child soldiers formed the basis of his debut novel "Beasts of No Nation" which was published in 2005 and was turned into an award-winning film in 2015.

It tells the story of Agu, a young boy in an unnamed West African country who is forced to become a boy soldier and fight in a bloody civil war. Under the influence of the Commandant, Agu is forced to leave his childhood behind – his family, his friends, his love of reading, his dreams of becoming a doctor – and instead becomes party to the crimes of war: killing, looting, rape and hunger.

The book, written in the first person, is notable for its unique direct and very immediate yet very simplistic style.

The first of the three extracts is the very beginning of the story. The second is a flashback to happier days from his childhood and the final extract is taken from near the end of the story when it seems there is almost no hope left for Agu.

Extract 1

It is starting like this. I am feeling itch like insect is crawling on my skin, and then my head is just starting to tingle right between my eye, and then I am wanting to sneeze because my nose is itching, and then air is just blowing into my ear and I am hearing so many thing: the clicking of insect, the sound of truck grumbling like one kind of animal, and then the sound of somebody shouting, TAKE YOUR POSITION RIGHT NOW! QUICK! QUICK QUICK! MOVE WITH SPEED! MOVE FAST OH! in voice that is just touching my body like knife.

I am opening my eye and there is light all around me coming into the dark through hole in the roof, crossing like net above my body. Then I am feeling my body crunched up like one small mouse in the corner when the light is coming on. The smell of rainwater and sweat is coming into my nose and I am feeling my shirt is so wet it is almost like another skin. I want to be moving, but my whole bone is paining me and my muscle is paining me like fire ant is just biting me all over my body. If I can be slapping myself to be making it go away I am doing it, but I cannot even move one finger. I am not doing anything.

Footstep is everywhere around me and making me to think that my father is coming to bring medicine to stop all of this itch and pain. I turn onto my back. The footstep is growing louder, louder, louder until I am hearing it even more than my own breathing or heart beating. Step slap, step slap, step slap, I am hearing getting louder, louder, louder and then shadow is coming into the light from under the door.

Somebody is knocking. KNOCK KNOCK. But I am not answering. Then they are angrying too much and just kicking so the

---

3 **to tingle** to feel itchy or uncomfortable – 17 **fire ant** *Feuerameise*

whole of this place is shaking and the roof is falling apart small small so that more light is coming in. And the wood every where is cracking until I am hearing PING PING and seeing screw falling from the door into bucket near my feets. The sound is fighting the wall, bouncing from here to there, through the net of light, until it is like the sound is pushing the door open so there is so much brightness. BRIGHTNESS! So much brightness is coming into my eye until I am seeing purple spot for long time. Then I am seeing yellow eye belonging to one short dark body with one big belly and leg thin like spider's own. This body is so thin that his short is just blowing around his leg like woman's skirt and his shirt is looking like dress the way it is hanging from his shoulder. His neck is just struggling too much to hold up his big head that is always moving one way or the other.

I am looking at him. He is looking at me. He is not surprising at all to be seeing me even if I am surprising for him, but his face is falling and becoming more dark. He is sniffing like dog and stepping to me. KPAWA! He is hitting me.

Again and again he is hitting me and each blow from his hand is feeling on my skin like the flat side of machete. I am trying to scream, but he is knocking the air from my chest and then slapping my mouth. I am tasting blood. I am feeling like vomiting. The whole place around us is shaking, just shaking rotten fruit from the shelf, just sounding like it will be cracking into many piece and falling on top of us. He is grabbing my leg, pulling it so hard that it is like it will be coming apart like meat, and my body is just sliding slowly from the stall out into the light and onto the mud.

In the light, my breath is coming back and using force to open my chest to make me to coughing and my eye to watering. The

---

4 **bucket** *Eimer* – 22 **to vomit** to be sick, to throw up

whole world is spreading before me and I am looking up to the gray
sky moving slowly slowly against the top leaf of all the tall tall Iroko
tree. And under this, many smaller tree is fighting each other to
climb up to the sunlight. All the leaf is dripping with rainwater and
shining like jewel or glass. The grasses by the road is so tall and green
past any color I am seeing before. This is making me to think of
jubilating, dancing, shouting, singing because Kai! I am saying I am
finally dead. I am thinking that maybe this boy is spirit and I should
be thanking him for bring ing me home to the land of spirits, but
before I can even be open ing my mouth to be saying anything, he
is leaving me on my back in the mud.

I can see the bottom of truck parking just little bit away from me.
Two truck is blocking up the whole road and more are parking on
the roadside. The piece of cloth covering them is so torn up and full
of hole and the paint is coming off to showing so much rust, like
blood, making me to thinking the truck is like wounding animal.
And around all the truck, just looking like ghost, are soldier. Some
is wearing camouflage, other is wearing T-shirt and jean, but it is
not mattering because all of the clothe is tearing and having big
hole. Some of them is wearing real boot and the rest is wearing
slipper. Some of them is standing at attention with their leg so
straight that it is looking like they do not have knee. Some of them
is going to toilet against the truck and other is going to toilet into
the grasses. Almost everybody is carrying gun.

The boy who is hitting me is running to the first truck. When he
is reaching the door, he is bending down with his back so straight
and his leg so straight. Only his head is moving back and forward,
left and right, on his neck. Then he is standing up and suddenly,
quick just like that, the door of the truck is swinging open and

---

1 **to spread** to stretch out – 18 **camouflage** [ˈkæməflɑːʒ] green and brown clothing used
by soldiers – 19 **to tear** to pull paper, cloth etc. into pieces

hitting the boy right in his big belly and he is just taking off like bird, flying in the air, and landing on his buttom in hole of water in the road. There is sound coming from all the other soldier. It is laughing sound.

I am lying here even if I am wanting to get up because my body is just paining me and I am fearing that if I am moving, somebody will be doing something very bad to me.

A man is coming down from the truck. He is looking like the leader. I am staring at the man and his jacket that is coming apart into many green string moving back and forward each time he is breathing in or out. He is wearing glove so dirty they are almost yellow or brown and his cap that he is holding in the sweaty place under his arm is flopping down because it is soaked almost all the way with his sweat.

I am watching him move from truck to truck. The truck is so old that the paint is falling off and the tire is so low that when he is kicking them, they are pressing in and out. All the other soldier is following each movement he is making; even all the one holding their gun ready to shoot is shifting his head to be watching him looking at every truck. He is moving slowly like important person to make sure that everybody looking at him is knowing he is chief. All of the other soldier is staring at him like he is king. I am staring also.

By the time this leader man is leaving the last truck, they are surrounding him and all of them are moving the same way he is moving. They are following him to me. Their shadow is surrounding me and their leg is like cage around me. Nobody is saying one word and the man is chewing the inside of his cheek just looking at me like I am ant or some insect like that. He is saying, so who is finding this thing? But nobody is answering.

---

13 **soaked** [soʊkt] very wet – 21 **chief** boss

Then he is saying louder, why is this thing here on the ground?

The boy who is finding me is now coming back from my shack with some banana just as black as the road. He is wiping fruit from his mouth with his hand and walking to this big man who is saying to him, Strika. Is it you who is finding this thing? And the little boy is nodding his head very hard like he is happy that the man is knowing it is him.

Enh! Strika? Is it you, the man is saying. Heyeye! Hmm! he is shouting and then he is turning to the other soldier and cursing them. So you mean of all of you GROWN MEN only this boy –one skinny little thing like this – is finding this thing here.

I am not moving and the leader man is throwing up his arm to the sky. He is shouting, where are you finding him, so hard that his voice is becoming high and sounding like it is sticking in his throat. Strika is pointing his arm at the shack. Is that right, the man is saying and shaking his head like he cannot be believing it at all at all. SSSSS! He is shouting, you. Where is Luftenant? Luftenant. LUFTENANT! And another voice is answering, he is in the bush.

The grasses is shaking and man is coming from there holding his trouser up with one hand and holding his gun with the other. His yellow skin is shining like gold and sweat is shining on his beard. He is running to us and stopping when he is coming to be looking at me like he is confusing too much. Then he is saluting very lazy, not like everybody else who is looking like they are not even able to bend anything.

Commandant Sah! he is shouting in voice that is even sounding like somebody whining. This man Commandant is saying, come here. Come here, until Luftenant is moving closer to Commandant who is shouting, JUST WHAT ARE YOU DOING? Luftenant is not saying anything. You don't know? Please Sah. I was shitting in

---

2 **shack** small house, cabin, hut – 17 **Luftenant** (*dial*) Lieutenant, a rank in the army

the bush. And Commandant is grabbing Luftenant's ear until the man is squeezing his face with so much pain. Open your ear and listen to me well well, Commandant is saying. If you are wanting to shit, you are not shitting on my time. Who are you? Just running into the bush like woman. If you are wanting to shit, you should be shitting right here on the road. You are not leaving this road for anything. Are you understanding me Luftenant? He is nodding, yes yes, and all the other soldier are trying not to be laughing by stomping their feet and coughing or pretending to sneeze.

Can you be telling me what this is, Commandant is saying and pointing to me. Why are you leaving Strika to bring him out?

Oh God. What am I doing, Luftenant is saying. He is spy oh. It is ambush oh. Let's just kill him and clear from this place.

SHUTUP YOUR MOUTH, Commandant is shouting. Who and who is asking you to speak? Idiot. If anybody is coming here, we will deal with them proper.

Then everybody is starting to laugh, even Commandant, and while this is happening I am seeing how Luftenant is looking like he is wanting to be killing Commandant. He is grumbling to himself and making his hand into fist.

Commandant is kneeling next to me and smiling so I am seeing how his teeths is in his mouth anyhow, just yellow with gap here and there. His gum is black and his eye is so red. His nose is coming out into a very round bulb at the tip which is sticking over his fat brown lip. He is stretching his glove to my face, grabbing it hard but also soft like he is caring for me, and then he is looking at all of the blood, and dirt, and mosquito bite, and mud I am having on me from dragging in the road. He is clicking his tongue and saying to Strika, are you trying to eat this one or what. And Strika is shaking his head no. Since he is finding me I can never hearing this boy speak.

---

9 **to sneeze** *niesen* – 12 **oh** (*NPidgin*) used for emphasis at the end of sentences – 24 **bulb** *here*: big, round shape

By now I am knowing who is Strika and Commandant and Luftenant. But there are so many person who is just not saying anything at all that I am wondering if they are even knowing how to speak. Commandant is turning to me. Do you want some water, he is saying softly, but I am not answering because I am floating on top of my body and just watching. The world is changing into many color around me and I am hearing the people speaking, but it is like different language. I am floating away like leaf in water until KPWISHA! I am feeling cold and more wet and then how my body is so heavy all around me.

Strika, Commandant is saying. Go and bring more water. Strika is running to the last truck and jumping up. Then Commandant is saying to me, are you hungry? Are you thirsty? And because I am feeling much better and my head is feeling more clear, I am touching my belly and nodding my head yes.

He is saying, well that is no problem. If you are wanting food, you will eat. And if you are wanting drink, you will drink, but that is having to wait until you are telling me your name. How can I be sitting down to eat with a man who I am not knowing his name? Are you hearing me? I am nodding to him again, but word is not able to be coming from my mouth.

You are having name is it not, he is saying and sticking his face into my own face. I am trying hard to remember, to be squeezing my thought for my name, but I am not getting anything. Now Commandant is getting angry and pointing to himself. My name is Commandant. Everybody is always calling me Commandant. What is everybody always calling you?

I am shaking my head trying to remember as Commandant is just reaching to his belt and showing me one black gun like that. I am wanting to cry and I am feeling like I am having to go to toilet, but I am knowing if I am doing this, he will be killing me just like that so I am shaking my head and looking at his red eye until I am remembering just like that how in my village everybody is calling

me Agu because that is what my father is calling me. I am whispering
Agu, my name is Agu because it is hard for me to be talking and
then I am seeing how Commandant is taking his hand from his gun
and smiling. Agu enh? They are calling you Agu. Well, that is what
I will be calling you, he is saying. And I am breathing again and my
head is not hurting so much because I am thinking, Glory be to God
in the Highest I am still living.

Commandant is having smile crawling slowly onto his face and
he is turning to his soldier and saying, see this one on the road. Do
you see him? And they are all shouting, YES YES while Commandant
is touching his beard and using his fingernail to pick all the scab and
cut from between the hairs. He is looking from soldier to soldier
and everybody is staying quiet.

BRING WATER EHN! he is just shouting and Strika is handing
him one small blue jerry can with red top. Commandant is taking
one dirty handkerchief from his breast pocket and wetting it with
some water. Then he is grabbing the back of my head and rubbing
my face saying, well, if you are going to be eating with man, then
you are having to be clean. I am feeling the water in all my scratch,
bite, and cut and it is stinging me too much. I am wanting to shout,
but he is smiling with his tongue in his teeths like he is finding and
cleaning old treasure. I am so thirsty.

[…]

---

11 **scab** a rough layer that forms over a wound – 15 **jerry can** metal container for storing
water or petrol

Extract 2

I am not bad boy. I am not bad boy. I am soldier and soldier is not bad if he is killing. I am telling this to myself because soldier is supposed to be killing, killing, killing. So if I am killing, then I am only doing what is right. I am singing song to myself because I am hearing too many voice in my head telling me I am bad boy. They are coming from all around me and buzzing in my ear like mosquito and each time I am hearing them, they are chooking my heart and making my stomach to turn. So I am singing,

> *Soldier Soldier*
> *Kill Kill Kill.*
> *That is how you live.*
> *That is how you die.*

This is my song that I am singing all of the time wherever we are going to be reminding myself that I am only doing what sol dier is supposed to be doing. But it is never working because I am always feeling like bad boy. So I am thinking, how can I be bad boy? Me, bad boy – somebody who is having life like I am having and fearing God the whole time.

I am learning how to read very early in my life from my mother and my father. When I am very small, before even my sister is born, I am always sitting with my mother on the floor of the kitchen and watching her washing all the plate. In the evening, I am always sitting on the floor just watching her with her buttom sticking high into the air and her breast touching her knee while she is working to make the kitchen so clean that not even fruit fly is wanting to put its egg inside.

---

8 **to chook** (*NPidgin*) to cause a sharp pain, to stab

I am liking to read so much that my mother is calling me professor. I am pulling her dress and she is saying to me, two more minute professor. Only two more minute. Then she is locking the door and holding my hand as we are walking to the main house.
Inside, my father is always just sleeping sleeping or listening to his radio, so we would be moving quietly, getting the matches from the wood table in the middle of the room and lighting the lamp just in case they are taking the light. All of this is making me to agitate because it is taking so long until finally she is coming to the bookshelf and pretending to search for just the right book. The shelf was having many book of different size and different color – some red, some yellow, some blue, and some brown – but the one I am always wanting her to pick, the only one that I am wanting to hear is the one that is holding all of the other book up, the big white Bible. I was so small and the book was so big that I am almost not even able to be carrying it. But I was enjoying how the cover is so soft, and how the letter saying HOLY BIBLE was made of gold. This was my favourite book because of how it is looking and because of all the story inside of it. Whenever my mother is touching it, I am shouting, that one, that one and she is saying, shhh don't be so loud or you will be waking your father. I was always sitting in her laps on our favourite chair and we are staring at the small small letter on the page. She was reading over my shoulder and I am feeling her lip moving in my ear as she was saying each word. My mother is reading very very slowly because she is not schoolteacher like my father who is knowing too much about book. She is not going to school for long enough like my father, but she was always saying, I am knowing enough to read the only book that is mattering. This is why Pastor is liking her so much.

---

8 **to agitate** to become worried or upset

She is reading to me about how Cain is killing his brother Abel, and how God is visiting Abraham, and about Jonah living in the fish. She was also reading about how God is making Job to suffer very much, but how He is rewarding him at the end, and how David is killing Goliath. Each time she is reading this story I would be thinking in my head that I am standing here looking at how all the army is shining with gold and bronze in the sun and how Goliath is laughing until David is cutting off his head. I am seeing all of these thing when she is reading and thinking that I am wanting to be warrior. And all the time my mother is reading I am pointing to each word and asking what is that what is that so she can be telling me and I can be learning. We were doing this every evening until my mother is saying, okay Agu it is enough now. My eye is tired.

When my mother is not there, I was going to the shelf to be reading The Bible myself. My mother was still reading to me every night, but I was also able to be reading by myself, and soon, when my father was coming back from work to be sitting in his short and singlet listening to the radio in his favourite chair, I was sitting with him and not my mother and I would be reading to him what I am teaching myself from The Bible. I was wanting to show him that I am big enough to be going to school so I can be learning everything that he is knowing that is making everybody in the village to like him so much. I was always asking him every day, tomorrow can I be going to school? Tomorrow can I go to school, and he was always saying to me, just wait just wait. Enh. Agu! Why are you wanting to grow so big so fast? Then I would be going to my mother to be begging her to help me go to school. I was wanting to go so much that each time I would be crying to her to make my father take me to school and she is saying to me that if I am crying like this, then at school they will just be laughing at me. So, when my father is

---

10 **warrior** a brave and experienced fighter – 18 **singlet** vest, sleeveless T-shirt

coming home, I was first asking him how is his own school that he is teaching and then I was asking him if I am big enough and he was telling me to take my right hand and put it over my head to touch my left ear, but I was too small to be doing that so he was telling me, Agu you are not ready yet.

Until one day, I am running to my father and saying, look, and then taking my hand over my head and touching my ear. He is smiling and saying, okay, and then the next day we are going to the primary school where everybody is wearing uniform that is red short and white shirt if you are boy and red skirt and white shirt if you are girl. I was looking at all of them holding one red notebook and Biro in their hand and standing in line not making any noise. The boys were all having head shaved and the girls were all having plaits so that everybody is looking the same. I wanted to be wearing uniform and carrying red notebook and Biro too much so I was just standing there agitating.

My father was taking me to Mistress Gloria who is the head teacher and asking her if I can be going to school, but she was asking, this one? Isn't he too small? And I was looking at how Mistress Gloria is having very fat belly and big cheek and I wanted to be saying, I am only too small because you are so big, but my father is saying, no. He is not small and Mistress Gloria is having to take me in.

Because my father was schoolteacher and my mother is always reading to me from The Bible, I was already reading when the other children are just trying to learn. I was the smartest person in my class, so smart that the only thing I am having to learn is writing. Mistress Gloria was seeing how smart I am and she is moving me up with the other people in primary one so I was just sitting on a bench with people bigger than me. When all of the other student

---

12 **biro** *Kugelschreiber* – 14 **plait** [plæt] braid (three pieces of hair twisted together)

are having their leg touch the ground while they are sitting, my own was just swinging back and forward in the air.

The school is just one big building with blackboard at the front of the dassroom. This is where Mistress Gloria is standing when she is teaching lesson. All of the class are having their lesson in this one room so that Mistress Gloria was teaching every class up to primary six. She was always holding one large wooden ruler that she would be using to hit you on the head if you are not behaving well. Sometimes during the day we are having quiet time where the younger people is having to put their head down on their desk and all the older one is having to copy their lesson in their notebook. I am always doing my lesson at home so during quiet time I am sitting and thinking about different thing. I always liked thinking about everything that I am reading in book until it is time to play. Even though I am learning with the older children, I am always playing with all my mates. I am having one very good friend who is having Engineer for father so they are some of the rich people in the village. My friend's name was Dike. He was tall past me even if we are the same age, but he was still my best friend.

But these thing are before the war and I am only remembering them like dream. I am seeing my school and all of my friend. I am seeing Mistress Gloria and her curly black wig of hairs that she was always shifting around because it is not staying on her head well well. Some people were hating Mistress Gloria and always making fun of her by pushing out their belly big and walking around like fat goat, but I am liking Mistress Gloria and she was liking me. She was always saying to me softly when I was leaving the classroom after helping her to clean up, Agu make sure you study book enh? If you are studying hard you can be going to the university to be Doctor or Engineer.

---

22 **wig** a covering for the head made of hair

All of this thing that she was always telling me are making me to happying because I was seeing how the Doctor and the Engineer is being treated. I was putting all this thing in my head and remembering them but not letting them be taking up too much of my time as I am young. So after talking with her like this each day, I was then going to play with all my friend in the schoolyard. I was having many friend in my village because all of the other children were thinking that I am nice boy and also I am the best at all of the game and all of the lesson we are learning. So they were all liking me and wanting to be my friend, but the person who was really liking me and who I was really liking was my best friend Dike. We are always doing everything together in the village. So after going from Mistress Gloria, I was going with Dike to be going behind the schoolyard with some of the other boy to be playing football in the dust with one flat ball that is never very good to kick or we are having the race that I am always winning and I was flying up and down the school yard even if I am only wearing slipper. I am liking school very much and always thinking about going until the war is coming and then they are stopping school because there is no more government.

I am always going to church every Sunday where I am first going to the Sunday school to be sitting outside under the shade of one big tree in the church compound with all of my mate and sometimes, if she is not causing too much trouble, my sister, to be listening to the women reading us more story from The Bible about Jesus and Joseph and Mary and telling us that we should watch out so that we are taking the hard road and not the easy road. And then we are saying prayer for forgiveness and the Our Father and also singing many song because God is liking music more than just talking so if we are singing, then He is listening to us well well. They are always telling us that God is liking children so much, that He is always watching us. Sometimes after Sunday school is finishing I am going into the big grey church and sitting with my mother and father who

are dressing in their nice clothe and listening to Pastor shouting and
sweating. I am feeling how the wood is chooking my buttom with
splinter and how the fan above us is shaking so much that it is
looking like it was going to fall and be cutting off my head. I was
always watching how the women would be dancing well well so that
their clothe is shaking and they are having to tie it and tie it again
and singing very loud when it is time to put their money in the
collection plate. And the men are just shuffling their feets and
bowing their head so their chin is touching their chest.

And on Sunday there are other thing that we are doing in my
village. When there is no school and no chore, all my friend and me
are making all kind of game to be playing. Sometimes, we are
playing that we are grown up and doing grown-up thing like driving
car and flying plane, or being Doctor or Boatman. And sometimes
we are playing that we are soldier like we are some times seeing in
movie and taking stick and using them as gun to be shooting at each
other and falling down each time to pretending we are dead. And
each time we are playing all this game we are having so much fun
and laughing and running and yelling all up and down the road of
the village. All the small small children are watching us and wanting
to be like us and even the grown people are watching us and even if
they are yelling at us to stop making so much noise, I am knowing
from the way that they are shouting through their teeths they are
trying not to be smiling because they are also wanting to be just like
us. So we were playing all this game then and thinking that to be a
soldier was to be the best thing in the world because gun is looking
so powerful and the men in movie are looking so powerful and
strong when they are killing people, but I am knowing now that to
be a soldier is only to be weak and not strong, and to have no food
to eat and not to eat whatever you want, and also to have people

---

3 **splinter** a small, thin, sharp piece of wood – 8 **collection plate** *Klingelbeutel*

making you do thing that you are not wanting to do and not to be doing whatever you are wanting which is what they are doing in movie. But I am only knowing this now because I am soldier now.

So I am singing to myself,

> *Soldier Soldier*
> *Kill Kill Kill.*
> *That is how you live.*
> *That is how you die.*

And I am remembering to myself that I am doing all of this thing before I am soldier and it is making me to feel better. If I am doing all of this good thing and now only doing what soldier is supposed to be doing, then how can I be bad boy?

Extract 3

It is night. It is day. It is light. It is dark. It is too hot. It is too cold.
It is raining. It is too much sunshine. It is too dry. It is too wet. But
all the time we are fighting. No matter what, we are always fighting.
All the time bullet is just eating everything, leaf, tree, ground, person
– eating them – just making person to bleed everywhere and there
is so much blood flooding all over the bush. The bleeding is making
people to be screaming and shouting all the time, shouting to father
and to mother, shouting to God or to Devil, shouting one language
that nobody is really knowing at all. Sometimes I am covering my
ear so I am not hearing bullet and shouting, and sometimes I am
shouting and screaming also so I am not hearing anything but my
own voice. Sometimes I am wanting to cry very loud, but nobody
is crying in this place. If I am crying, they will be looking at me
because soldier is not supposed to be crying.

All the time, we are sick and going to toilet, shitting water. We are
hungry too and living off anything we can find. Lizard, we are eating
them. Insect, we are eating them or even better, if we are finding
them, we are eating rat and every other kind of bush animal.
Sometimes we are eating this leaf or that leaf, but leaf is what is
always making my belly to turn so I am not eating it so much. Meat
is also making my stomach to turn because we are not able to use
too much fire to cook it because if we are using too much fire, then
the enemy will be seeing us and shooting us dead from where they
are hiding. I am always hungry, so hungry that I am always dreaming
of chicken and how I will be eating it, how I will be crunching its
beak and eating even the feather. I am so hungry I can be eating
wood if it is making me to hungry less, but it is only hurting my
belly and making me to vomit and shit. I am so hungry I can even

---

17 **lizard** small reptile with a long tail – 27 **beak** hard part of a bird's mouth

be eating my skin small by small if it is not making me to bleed to death. I am so hungry that I am wanting to die, but if I am dying, then I will be dead.

But there is so much bombing and bombing and shelling and shelling and sending helicopter to come and shine light on us and kill us. All the time, the ground is shaking and the tree is shaking and the air is smelling of smoke or the air is beating in your ear BOTU BOTU BOTU and you are not even having one second to be thinking anything. So much time pass us now. I am not seeing road or village or woman or children for too long. I am only seeing war, one evil spirit sitting in the bush just having too much happiness because all the time he is eating what he wants to eat – us – and seeing what he is wanting to see – killing – so he is just laughing GBWEM! GBWEM! GBWEM!

All of our truck is gone, just bombed away, so we are having to walk everywhere now, and there is not so many of us anymore. People are just dying like this every day. One boy named Hope is dying, just burning up in the fire of bomb that is hitting truck. One man we are calling Dagger is dying because he is stepping on mine and it is just chewing his whole body to many piece like termite is chewing wood. And Griot is dying from malaria making him to shaking shaking, and Preacher is dying holding his Bible in one hand and his leg in the other screaming to God, come take me come take me. People are dying just like that every day. Everyone I am knowing is dying. And even all the soldier whose name I am not knowing is dying. In the middle of this war, I am even missing some of them. I am even missing some of them.

Commandant is helping some people to be dying. Already he is shooting three people he is calling traitor, including Driver who is trying to run away because he is having no more truck to be driving.

---

4 **to shell** to attack with bombs – 29 **traitor** sb who is not loyal to a country, a group etc.

After Commandant is shooting Driver, he is laughing laughing and talking to himself and not even listening to anyone. Not even Rambo who is new Luftenant. When I am seeing all of this, all of this bombing bombing, killing killing, and dying dying, I am thinking to myself that now, as we are in this bush, only ant is still making and living. I am wishing I am ant.

Now we are just living underground in trench that we are digging in the red mud and just living inside it like one kind of snake or rat. When it is dry, we are happying because there is no water anywhere and we can just be fighting war. When it is raining? ah! It is so terrible. So terrible. It is like living in gutter. Sometimes water is coming up to my belly and I am just looking at my reflection staring at me everywhere I am going. We are staying in this place for too long. I am tired and hungry and I am wanting to leave.

There is so much mist that is wrapping around people like extra shirt. No shooting still for today and I am wanting to think, HEYA! WAR IS OVER! WAR IS OVER! but then I am think ing, is it really over? This whiteness that is hanging around all of us and making it hard to breathing is making me to feel like somebody is wanting to fly into my chest and close my nose with cotton. My feets are staying in the water all night so I am feeling they are curling at the end like the feets of rat. Some of the men are sleeping and hugging themself against the wall of the trench with their shirt on their head to be protecting them from the rain. They are shivering because there is cool wind that is coming through the whole place. lt is hard not to be stepping on them because they are just appearing quickly quickly from the mist. One second everything is all white around me and then I am kicking foot that is just appearing and the man is screaming in his sleep but not waking up. I am learning to see where the heat from body is making it less thick so I am walking carefully

---

7 **trench** *(Schützen-)Graben* – 24 **to shiver** to shake – 27 **mist** *Nebel*

when I am seeing this. Some of the men are awake because they are on guard all night and I am moving gegerly gegerly to not be disturbing them.

Strika is standing outside Commandant's HQ which is only just the trench, but with one blue cloth covering with leaf so he is not getting as wet as the rest of us. Strika is holding gun that is so heavy in his hand it is pulling the right side of his body to the ground. We are looking at each other for long time and then I am bringing my hand to be beating away the mist. I am not liking Strika's eye because they are too red and his teeths because they are too brown and his head because it is big, but he is my friend even if he is looking ugly. He is giving me the gun and then walking past me.

I am stepping inside HQ to see Commandant sleeping on his crate with his back against the mud wall and his boot stretching into the muddy water. Cigarette and ash is floating in the water around him and the whole room is smelling of smoke. I am taking deep breath to be drinking it all in because it is somehow making my body to full so I am not feeling as hungry.

His beard is growing so thick now that it is almost covering his whole chin and cheek. When he is breathing out, the hairs is shaking with his breath. Commandant is looking like wild man and behaving like madman. I am thinking of him running naked through the bush with only his big beard reaching down to his feets and it is making me want to laugh, but I am too hungry. Laughing is making my belly to hurt too much. Commandant is fearing the other soldier so much now that he is saying it is always good to be sleeping with one eye open. That is why either Strika or myself is always standing outside when he is sleeping. I am his one eye. Strika is his other.

Come on. Out of my way, Rambo's head is following his voice out of the mist while his spit is spraying onto my face. He is stepping

---

2 **gegerly** (*NPidgin*) carefully – 4 **HQ** Headquarters

from the whiteness to stand right in front of me. I am seeing him with his gun hanging on his shoulder. My belly is tighting and my neck is becoming stiff. I am holding the gun Strika is giving to me.

Commandant is sleeping, I am saying to Rambo. Well wake him up, he is saying back. I am stepping in front of him and kicking water in his boot. He is tiring so don't be bothering him, I am saying. My leg is shaking shaking and my feets are too too cold. Out of my way, Rambo is saying again and stepping right so I am holding my gun tighter and stepping in front of him. His boot is squishing the mud. No he is resting, I am saying.

Rambo is bending down so I am seeing his face and his beard that is growing thick and black. Listen you small boy. Get out of the way. We are not playing game. I am not remembering the last time I am playing game.

What is all of this noise, Commandant is saying. Sah it is me, Rambo is answering. Idiot can't you see I am sleeping. Enhen now Sah I can see. Then shutup and go back to your post. No Sah I am not doing that anymore Sah. And why not? Because we are leaving Sah. WHO AND WHO IS LEAVING? Commandant is shouting and then I am hearing him laughing quietly to himself from the shadow of his HQ.

In front of me, Rambo is swallowing so hard that I am feeling it in my own throat. And from the back of the HQ, Commandant's laughing is growing louder and louder until I am feeling him standing right behind me. He is pushing me aside with his arm and I am hitting rock in the wall. My shoulder is beginning to hurt. Who is leaving. Idiot. Go back to your post. You are leaving when I say leave. Understood? No Sah, never, Rambo is saying. We are going, Rambo is saying. I no want trouble oh, he is saying. Who is this we enh, Commandant is saying and laughing. You are the only one

---

2 **belly** stomach – 2 **to tight** (*eigentlich* **to tighten**) to become tense from fear or anger

stupid enough – I AM GOING, one voice is shouting. I AM
GOING TOO. AND ME, AND ME, AND ME the voice keep
yelling from the mist softer and softer until the farthest person is
shouting small small, saying and me. Rambo is sliding his finger to
the trigger of his gun and I am sliding my finger to my own trigger
because I am fearing what Commandant will be doing to me if I am
not protecting him, but then I am remembering how much he is
hurting me when he is chooking me and I am saying never. Never
will I be feeling sorry for him. Never will I be helping him. I am
lowering my gun.

See! We are going, Rambo is shouting to Commandant. Then he
is just taking his gun and shooting him. Only one shot just right in
the chest and I am seeing Commandant looking down to his chest
with his whole mouth open like he is screaming. But no sound is
coming out. He is not saying anything. And then his body is just
falling and making the water that is running down the trench red
like that.

Rambo is stopping his shaking and is puffing out his chest.
Rambo is looking at me and I am looking at him. He is looking at
me for long time and then he is just turning and climbing up wall
and I am hearing his boot crunching the leaf near my head. Then I
am looking up and hearing how all of the soldier is climbing up out
of the trench and I am hearing Rambo shouting, COME ON!
COME ON QUICK QUICK QUICK! MOVE FAST OH! MOVE
WITH SPEED! HOME HOME! WE ARE GOING HOME! I am
looking at Commandant and then I am climbing out of the trench.
I am tired and hungry and I am wanting to go home.

© Uzodinma Iweala

Text 3: Trial speech

by Ken Saro-Wiwa (1995)

Ken Saro-Wiwa was a Nigerian writer and political and environmental activist. He was a member of the Ogoni people, an ethnic minority whose homeland, Ogoniland, lies in the oil-rich Niger Delta. The Delta covers 20,000 km² and is home to approximately 20 million people, of which around 10% are Ogoni. The Delta is an important ecosystem containing one of the highest concentrations of biodiversity on the planet. It includes coastal areas, islands, mangrove swamps and rainforests.

Multinational oil companies started oil production in the Delta in 1958 and Nigeria is now Africa's largest oil producer. A huge network of pipelines connecting various oil and gas fields crisscrosses the Delta. However, according to Amnesty International, "the Niger Delta suffers from an epidemic of oil spills." Every year there are hundreds of oil spills that damage the environment and destroy the lives of the people living there. As a result the Ogoniland region suffers from extremely high levels of pollution.

In the 1990s Ken Saro-Wiwa campaigned for greater rights for his people. He led a nonviolent campaign against the environmental destruction of his homeland by the oil industry. In May 1994 he was arrested on false charges of incitement to murder and sentenced to death. The following text is a speech made by Saro-Wiwa during his trial. He was executed in November 1995.

My lord,

We all stand before history. I am a man of peace, of ideas. Appalled
by the denigrating poverty of my people who live on a richly
endowed land, distressed by their political marginalization and
economic strangulation, angered by the devastation of their land,
their ultimate heritage, anxious to preserve their right to life and to
a decent living, and determined to usher to this country as a whole
a fair and just democratic system which protects everyone and every
ethnic group and gives us all a valid claim to human civilization, I
have devoted my intellectual and material resources, my very life,
to a cause in which I have total belief and from which I cannot be
blackmailed or intimidated. I have no doubt at all about the ultimate
success of my cause, no matter the trials and tribulations which I
and those who believe with me may encounter on our journey. Nor
imprisonment nor death can stop our ultimate victory.

I repeat that we all stand before history. I and my colleagues are
not the only ones on trial. Shell is here on trial and it is as well that
it is represented by counsel said to be holding a watching brief. The
Company has, indeed, ducked this particular trial, but its day will
surely come and the lessons learnt here may prove useful to it for
there is no doubt in my mind that the ecological war that the
Company has waged in the Delta will be called to question sooner
than later and the crimes of that war be duly punished. The crime
of the Company's dirty wars against the Ogoni people will also be
punished.

---

2 **appalled** [əˈpɔːld] shocked – 3 **denigrating** *here:* insulting, disrespectful – 4 **to endow**
[enˈdaʊ] to supply, provide – 4 **marginalization** *(politische) Ausgrenzung* – 6 **heritage**
[ˈherɪtɪdʒ] *Erbschaft* – 7 **to usher** to bring – 10 **to devote** *widmen* – 12 **to blackmail** to put
pressure on *(erpressen)* – 13 **trials and tribulations** *(phrase)* pain, problems – 18 **brief** *here:*
instructions – 22 **Delta** Niger River delta in southern Nigeria, an area rich in oil and which
has suffered much pollution

On trial also is the Nigerian nation, its present rulers and those who assist them. Any nation which can do to the weak and disadvantaged what the Nigerian nation has done to the Ogoni, loses a claim to independence and to freedom from outside influence. I am not one of those who shy away from protesting injustice and oppression, arguing that they are expected in a military regime. The military do not act alone. They are supported by a gaggle of politicians, lawyers, academics and businessmen, all of them hiding under the claim that they are only doing their duty, men and women too afraid to wash their pants of urine.

We all stand on trial, my lord, for by our actions we have denigrated our country and jeopardized the future of our children. As we subscribe to the sub-normal and accept double standards, as we lie and cheat openly, as we protect injustice and oppression, we empty our classrooms, denigrate our hospitals, fill our stomachs with hunger and elect to make ourselves the slaves of those who aspire to higher standards, pursue the truth, and honor justice, freedom, and hard work. I predict that the scene here will be played and replayed by generations yet unborn. Some have already cast themselves in the role of villains, some are tragic victims, some still have a chance to redeem themselves. The choice is for each individual.

I predict that the denouement of the riddle of the Niger delta will soon come. The agenda is being set at this trial. Whether the peaceful ways I have favored will prevail depends on what the oppressor decides, what signals it sends out to the waiting public.

---

6 **oppression** unfair treatment that limits sb's freedom – 8 **gaggle** large group, crowd – 12 **to jeopardize** [ˈdʒepə-daɪz] to endanger, to risk – 17 **to aspire to** to aim for – 23 **denouement** [dəɪˈnuːmɑ̃] end (result), climax

In my innocence of the false charges I face here, in my utter conviction, I call upon the Ogoni people, the peoples of the Niger delta, and the oppressed ethnic minorities of Nigeria to stand up now and fight fearlessly and peacefully for their rights. History is
5 on their side. God is on their side. For the Holy Quran says in Sura 42, verse 41: "All those that fight when oppressed incur no guilt, but Allah shall punish the oppressor." Come the day.

---

6 **to incur** to experience, to suffer

Text 4: The Agonist

(for Ken Saro-Wiwa & the Ogoni 8)

by Ogaga Ifowodo (2005)

The Nigerian poet, scholar and lawyer Ogaga Ifowodo was born in
1966 and has been awarded several prizes for his internationally
renowned poetry. In 1997 Ifowodo was arrested for calling for stronger
sanctions against the military dictatorship of Sani Abache. He was
imprisoned without trial with other Nigerian human rights activists,
writers and journalists. He was released in 1998.

"Memory Was His Saviour and His Death" forms the second part
of Ogaga Ifowodo's poem "The Agonist", first published in his poetry
collection "The Oil lamp". The poems in this collection focus on the
ecological destruction of the Niger Delta region and are a bitter
criticism of the oil industry and the pollution it is causing to the land
the Ogoni people call home, making it ultimately 'unlivable'.

"Memory Was His Saviour and His Death" is a tribute to Ken Saro-
Wiwa.

2) Memory Was His Saviour and His Death

Memory was his saviour. And his death!
He remembered the swamps and the rivers,
the fish shivering in a choked net,
the colony of creeks and mudskippers

founded by retreating tides. And the farms
swollen with roots and bulbs. He remembered
a bounty whose splendour wrote psalms
chanted by the peasant to winds and birds.

Memory was his saviour and his death.

He had known the floods, the tides and the waves
that softened the land and brought the fish home;
at one with nature's lore, they left no graves.

He came to know the black springs of the fuel oil
spewing liquid fire from iron pythons
coiled like rigs of death round their love and toil;

he came to know cities floated on the oil
plundered from the land under his feet, where
councils held in big halls to share the spoils

and memory became his saviour from death

---

3 **swamp** *Sumpfgebiet* – 5 **creek** stream – 5 **mudskipper** type of fish found in swamps –
6 **to retreat** to move back – 8 **bounty** *here:* a large harvest, plentiful supply – 13 **lore** *here*:
tradition, convention – 15 **python** large snake – 16 **toil** hard work, struggle

when the housewife stood aghast by her plot
of cassava and herbs swallowed by slick

when trees, fish and animals in mourning
surrendered to acid rain and gas poison

5   when the canoe paddling children to school
capsized far from bridge or motorway

when the army invaded the village
shooting bombing burning raping laughing!

when the commander of the mob boasted
10   two hundred and twenty-one ways of killing,

memory became his saviour from the death
when he bore witness to the rape and the shame!

---

1 **aghast** [əˈgæst] filled with horror – 2 **cassava** *Maniokstrauch* – 3 **in mourning** grieving sb
who has died

Make notes here on what this section has contributed to
your bigger picture of "Voices of Africa – Nigeria"

3 Challenges in modern Nigeria

Introduction

Despite all the progress the nation has made and its status as the largest economy in Africa, Nigeria with its estimated population of around 200 million inhabitants from a variety of ethnic, religious and social backgrounds still faces massive challenges. The country is divided along many lines: it is a religiously diverse society and the population is roughly equally divided between Muslims and Christians. Since the early 2000s the country has suffered sectarian violence by the terrorist group Boko Haram and although the government has recently had some success in pushing back against the group, the North still frequently suffers from attacks and abductions. Tensions along ethnic lines persist too and for centuries there has been conflict between cattle herders (mainly the Fulani and Hausa people) and farmers in central Nigeria.

In terms of natural resources Nigeria is a very rich country with huge reserves of oil and gas as well as other minerals. However, it is also one of the poorest countries due to overpopulation, corruption and illegal affairs. Almost half of Nigeria's population lives in extreme poverty, a higher proportion even than in India. Poverty is leading people to leave rural areas and search for a better existence in cities, leading to overcrowding and the expansion of slums. It is also having the effect that highly skilled, well-educated Nigerians are leaving the country to go abroad ("brain drain"). Literacy rates are cause for concern too: over a third of Nigeria's adult population is unable to read or write. There is also high gender inequality. Child marriage is common in certain areas, and domestic violence and female genital mutilation are regarded as socially acceptable in many parts of society.

Nevertheless there is technical expansion in the country. Nearly every person in the bigger towns and cities owns and regularly uses a smartphone. Nigeria's international value and enormous expertise in digitalization, computer science and information technology is fast becoming one of the most prosperous sectors of industry.

Tasks

1. Listen to the NPR podcast Malnutrition Is Killing Nigeria's Children Because of Food Shortage (find it online, see the first page of this book). Then:
   a) **Summarize which three factors have contributed to the food shortage in Northern Nigeria.**
   b) **Consider which measures you would implement to improve the situation.**
2. Can information technology and social media help Nigeria to overcome its (social) difficulties and problems?

Text 1: Join us or die: the birth of Boko Haram

by Andrew Walker (The Guardian, 2016)

Founded by Mohammed Yusuf in 2002 the Islamic militant terrorist organization Boko Haram has been terrorizing Nigeria's northern regions for nearly two decades. The name, usually translated as "Western education is forbidden" has sometimes been referred to as the Nigerian Taliban. Boko Haram does not accept Nigeria's political system. Instead its aim is to establish an Islamic state based on sharia law. The violence has forced millions of Nigerians to become displaced. Thousands live in refugee camps or have left the country to become refugees in Europe in search of a safer life. Tens of thousands of people have been killed in suicide bombings and other attacks. There have also been mass abductions, the most reported of which occurred in 2014 when 276 girls were kidnapped from their school in Chibok.

The following article, published in The Guardian focuses on the founding and development of the group and provides background on some of the most important people in its hierarchy as well as its motivations.

How the tattered remnants of an Islamist sect transformed into a relentless terrorist army that Nigeria cannot defeat

In February 2009, I was at a motor park in Maraba, a satellite of the Nigerian capital Abuja, looking for motorcyclists wearing dried vegetables on their heads. The Nigerian Police Force had recently tightened laws requiring drivers and passengers of motorcycles to wear helmets. In the case of motorcycle taxis – known as *achabas* in northern Nigeria – drivers would now have to provide helmets for their passengers. There was an uproar. Everyone knew that taking a trip on an *achaba* could be a dangerous thing; the drivers had a reputation for recklessness. But many Nigerians did not like the new rules.

Above all, the law gave the police an opportunity for extortion. One motorcycle taxi driver told me it was going to cost him 10,000 naira (around £40) to buy two helmets. As he made between 300 and 400 naira per day (less than £2), there was no way he could afford to obey the new law. Everyone knew what would happen. The police would set up flying checkpoints, near markets, motor parks and busy thoroughfares. They would swoop down on motorcyclists, flailing sticks and canes as the riders madly accelerated out of their traps.

People who drive *achabas* are close to the bottom of society. They are men (and *only* men) without much formal education, often without any other marketable skill. Many sleep rough, under bridges or awnings, some sleep on their motorcycles, guarding their source of income. Their passengers are also mostly poor. The vast number of *achabas* on the roads is a symptom of Nigeria's economic problems. The new helmet law was, in the minds of most, just another squeeze on people already in perilous circumstances.

---

9 **uproar** great complaining – 11 **recklessness** *here*: dangerous driving – 13 **extortion** forcing sb to pay money by threatening them – 19 **thoroughfare** [ˈθɜːroʊfer] major road, highway – 24 **awning** *Markise* – 28 **perilous** dangerous, risky

When the regulations came into force, something strange happened. As hardly anyone had helmets to wear, *achaba* drivers took to the streets in all manner of improvised headgear. There were pictures in the press of people wearing paint cans and buckets; but
5 best of all were riders wearing hollowed-out watermelons and calabash bowls – rustic utensils made out of dried gourds that, before the advent of plastic, were ubiquitous as water vessels.

These *achaba* drivers had stood up against barely disguised official extortion. Their resistance was characteristically subversive.
10 But most Nigerians simply added the new legislation to the long list of things that made their lives difficult – then they prayed, hoped the police would quickly lose interest and carried on as normal.

In one part of the country, however, this cat-and-mouse game between police and Nigerian motorists would have much more
15 serious consequences. In Maiduguri, the capital of the north-eastern Borno state, enforcement of the helmet law caused an incident that would spark a violent conflict between the police and members of a radical Islamist sect that was then unknown to the world. This, in turn, would pitch Nigeria into war.

20 ■

Two years later, I watched as a slight young man entered the office of Maiduguri's Special Armed Robbery Squad. The building is known locally as "The Crack", ostensibly because it houses the elite police force. It is also a place from where, once a person falls in, they
25 might never emerge.

---

6 **calabash** *Flaschenkürbis* – 6 **gourd** [gɔːrd] hard-shelled fruit, like pumpkin –
7 **ubiquitous** [juːˈbɪkwətəs] existing everywhere – 9 **subversive** working against authority
(e.g. government) – 25 **to emerge** to come back out from

The young man, whose name was Mohammed Zakariyya, was led inside by two plainclothes officers. He had been arrested a few days before, after the car he was driving was stopped at a police checkpoint. He was thin and looked to be barely more than a teenager. His long pink, kaftan-like shirt was dirty and flecked with small spots of dried blood.

"They discovered the weapons we had hidden underneath the seat," Zakariyya told me and my fellow BBC journalist, Abdullahi Kaura Abubakar. When his companion was ordered out of the vehicle to let the police search it, he tried to drive off. The Police Mobile Force officers opened fire, killing him. (The red hatchback, now full of holes, sat in the yard of the Borno police headquarters.)

Zakariyya said that he had been on three arms smuggling missions. Each time, he and his accomplices drove 120km out of Maiduguri to meet a man who ferried weapons in a canoe downriver from the mountainous border with Cameroon. Each time, he brought them half-a-dozen AK-47s and a handful of boxes of ammunition. They loaded the car, then Zakariyya drove it through Maiduguri to a large house in the suburbs of Damaturu, the capital of the neighbouring state of Yobe.

The men he was working for had approached Zakariyya at the end of 2010 while he was selling shoes and phone chargers. "They used to preach in the open, so everyone was aware of who they were," he said.

"They" were members of the hardline Islamist sect that had established itself between 2005 and 2009 at a compound in Maiduguri's Railway district. Known as Boko Haram, which translates as "Western education is forbidden", the group had gradually brought more and more people under its influence.

---

2 **plainclothes** not wearing uniform – 11 **hatchback** *Kombi*

The man we had come to Maiduguri to speak with was a member who called himself Abu Dujana – his nom de guerre was taken from one of the companions of the prophet Muhammad. He described the atmosphere of the sect's Maiduguri headquarters in cult-like terms. The pace of life inside was dictated by the charismatic leader Mohammed Yusuf, who set and enforced strict standards of religious practice. "Yes, I lived there," Abu Dujana said proudly. "There wasn't a mosque like this in the whole of the country, where you could go and attain as much knowledge."

On 20 February 2009, members of the sect were travelling to a funeral in a large group. The convoy was made up of many motorbikes, and the police stopped them. The police were part of a state-wide task force, named Operation Flush and set up in 2005 to combat political thugs who had run amok in elections two years before. The dispute between the group and the police about their refusal to wear helmets became heated. Some reports of the exchange say that the police shot first, others that a member of the group disarmed a policeman and tried to use his weapon on the other police officers. In any case, the police opened fire, and several people in the travelling funeral party were killed and wounded.

This was not the first time that Operation Flush had crossed paths with Boko Haram, and the group's leadership had already concluded that the purpose of the Joint Task Force was to harass them directly. In the weeks following this encounter, Yusuf made a series of speeches, circulated widely on tapes and DVDs and over Bluetooth connections, calling on Muslims to prepare to "come to Jihad". This, he said, included "material preparation such as learning shooting, buying rifles and bombs, as well as training the Islamic

---

2 **nom de guerre** [ˌnɒmdəˈgeː] (French) name under which a person fights – 14 **thug** a violent person – 14 **to run amok** (*phrase*) to behave uncontrollably in order to disrupt – 23 **to harass** [həˈræs] to disturb or attack

Soldiers to fight the infidels. You should sacrifice your souls, your homes, your cars and your motorcycles for the sake of Allah."

Yusuf also had a large farm in Bauchi state, which he used as a base. The state government responded to these speeches by ordering the police to raid the farm, capturing hundreds of Boko Haram members and killing several more. The police laid siege to the sect's headquarters in the Ibn Taymiyyah mosque compound in Maiduguri. "They did not engage us fully, but tried to provoke us, driving along the side of the compound in a jeep," Dujana told me. "We waited until we had our chance and then we took it."

When they saw the state's forces had pulled back and commenced shooting at them from a distance, the men inside armed themselves and broke out of the compound. Dujana said they split into groups – he led one detachment, which roamed the city looking for military and police units to attack. For four days Boko Haram rampaged through the streets of Maiduguri. As well as killing police and soldiers, they slaughtered scores of civilians who were caught out in the open, slitting their throats like animals.

As the authorities re-established control of the town, Mohammed Yusuf was captured by the military. He was interrogated in front of journalists who filmed it with their phones. He was then handed over to the police. Within minutes, Yusuf was dead – shot, the police said, while trying to escape. Nobody believed this. Yusuf's bullet-ridden body was then displayed to journalists, who took pictures.

This was just the beginning of a tide of violence that has left thousands of people dead and at least 1.5 million people displaced from their homes. Seven years after Yusuf's killing, the war between Boko Haram and the Nigerian state has changed and developed.

---

1 **infidel** unbeliever, sb who does not believe the same as the majority – 1 **to sacrifice** to give up sth valuable – 5 **to raid** *here: eine Razzia durchführen* – 6 **to lay siege to** (*phrase*) to block off and attack – 17 **to slaughter** to kill a lot of people in a very brutal or violent way

From late 2014 to early 2015, the sect controlled an estimated 70 % of Borno state – the authorities, meanwhile, seemed incapable of dislodging it.

After his election in 2015, President Muhammadu Buhari of the All Progressives Congress party tried to reinvigorate the military leadership by replacing a number of top generals. This, he hoped, would bolster the state's response to Boko Haram. By August 2015, the military had reversed many of the group's gains and pushed it back to more remote areas. But the war is by no means finished.

In November, during attacks 48 hours apart, suicide bombers killed scores in the eastern city of Yola and Kano in the north, targets that lie hundreds of miles apart. These attacks show the extent of the group's reach, even outside the area it once controlled. There have been continual, under-reported, skirmishes in the border regions of north-east Nigeria. Just last Friday, on 29 January, the group launched an attack on Dalori, a small town close to Maiduguri. As many as 80 people were killed. Witnesses said they heard the screams of dying children as their houses burned down around them. These attacks are in spite of Buhari's announcement in December that the war was "technically over".

■

Yusuf's group did not appear out of nowhere. Even before the open war between Boko Haram and the state, it had been growing. Among its ranks were people from all levels of society, from street kids and traders, to disaffected students and wealthy businessmen.

Many of the young men and women came from the University of Maiduguri, where the elite of the 1990s sent their children to be

---

3 **to dislodge** to remove, to force out – 5 **to reinvigorate** to give new energy to –
7 **to bolster** to make stronger – 14 **skirmish** [ˈskɜːmɪʃ] short, small fight

educated. The institution was famed for the hedonism of its students, who indulged in ritual displays of wealth. The young sons of the elite would compete to be "King of Campus": the winner racked up the highest expense on parties. The "naira spray" was a particularly fashionable form of celebration, much seen during the oil boom of the 1970s: to honour a talented musician, dancer or a pretty girl, one of these wealthy young men would scatter a rain of currency that the object of their approval would then pick up off the floor.

To some, this fetishisation of money was an example of the injustice and immorality at the heart of the state. Disaffected students and university dropouts gravitated towards the youth wing of a Salafi group at a mosque in Maiduguri. Among them were the nephew of the governor of Yobe state, the son of the state secretary of Borno and five sons of a prominent businessman who had made his money through state contracts. These young men were drawn to the Salafists, who preached that such spiritual corruption was the cause of Borno's ills. Many of them burned their university certificates when they joined.

One man saw the potential of these young radicals, born into privilege. His name was Mohammed Yusuf.

Yusuf had been travelling around the north-east, preaching, making contacts and winning a following since the mid-1990s. He was a charismatic speaker who had no trouble attracting an audience. His radical ideas about the infidel state of Nigeria resonated with many people. He gave fiery orations at mosques and debated with other Islamic scholars on local television and radio.

According to his supporters, Yusuf was one of thousands of Almajiri children – religious students who beg on the streets for a

---

1 **hedonism** ['hedənɪzəm] seeking pleasure as a way of life – 12 **to gravitate to(wards)** to be attracted by – 22 **to preach** to give religious speeches – 26 **fiery oration** passionate, public speech

living. But by the early 2000s he had found a place as a leader of the youth wing of a Salafist group at Maiduguri's popular Alhaji Muhammadu Ndimi mosque.

Yusuf told his followers that Muslims who participated in any form of democratic system were apostates and should be killed by the faithful. The wellspring of corruption, he concluded, was the education system put in place during and after colonial rule by Christian Britain. He preached in busy towns on market days (rather than on Fridays, a breach of tradition that angered the Islamic authorities), where he picked up many followers.

In the years before the 2009 uprising, observers were shocked at the extent of Yusuf's influence, which spread deep into the border regions. Anthropologist Gerhard Müller-Kosack spent years studying a village in the Mandara mountains, near the border with Cameroon. He said the village changed "virtually overnight". When he visited for the last time in 2008, what surprised him most were the women: "Suddenly they were there in the full covering. It was the women at the forefront of the change." During their years in the village, Müller-Kosack and his wife had started a school. He had collected donations from friends and colleagues to buy textbooks. The last time he visited, he found the school abandoned: "All the books had been burned – the young women, it was they who made a pile of them and burned them in front of the school."

■

From the very beginning, Yusuf was preparing his followers for conflict. Among the first generation of supporters were many ideologues willing to unleash violence on the state, innocent

---

5 **apostate** [əˈpɑːsteɪt] a person who gives up his religion – 6 **wellspring** source, cause – 9 **breach** break – 21 **to abandon** to leave a place forever – 27 **to unleash** to release, to set loose

civilians, the Muslim establishment and anyone they declared to be unbelievers. They formed a "counter elite", united by resentment of years of secular rule in Nigeria. These men dreamed of a sharia wonderland, and believed it would come to Nigeria through
5 unremitting bloodshed.

Before the 2009 uprising, the Salafists associated with the Ndimi mosque had already made one disastrous attempt at creating an Islamic state. In 2003, a man named Muhammad Ali, who had tired of Yusuf's slow approach to building a movement, led a band of 200
10 young men and women out into the wilderness to start society anew. They ended up in the borderlands of Yobe state, near the dry river bed between Nigeria and the Republic of Niger, at a place called Kanamma. They were determined to shun the corrupt world and create a new land of Islamic purity.

15 This group of aggressive, iconoclastic city-dwellers soon came into conflict with the people who already lived in the place they tried to settle. Indeed, conflict was what they sought. They dug defensive preparations in a wooded grove near a water source. They raided local police stations and government buildings to get weapons, and
20 to provoke a reaction, which duly came. After a brief siege, the military overran and destroyed the camp. The group's members were mostly wiped out. A few survivors escaped north, over the border to Niger, where some can still be found. Others slunk back to Maiduguri.

25 The military crackdown attracted international attention because the group dubbed itself the "Nigerian Taliban". But, at the time, the US embassy concluded that it had no links to al-Qaida.

---

3 **sharia** the holy laws of Islam – 5 **unremitting bloodshed** never-ending killing and violence – 13 **to shun** to keep away from – 15 **iconoclastic** [aɪˌkɑːnəˈklæstɪk] criticizing or attacking established beliefs and traditions – 18 **grove** small wood, forested area

Yusuf had not joined the Kanamma uprising. Still, after the group was crushed, he went into self-imposed exile in Saudi Arabia to escape accusations that he had anything to do with it. It is thought that, while he was there, he made links with like-minded Salafi preachers and secured their support. But after a year, he was back in Maiduguri.

On his return, in 2005, Yusuf began to rebuild his own community, establishing the Ibn Taymiyyah mosque and compound in the Railway district of Maiduguri on land bought with the help of his father-in-law. This location, in the heart of the state capital, was key to the group's new incarnation. By embedding themselves in the town rather than the wilderness, the group had many more avenues for recruitment and funding. The population of Maiduguri has risen dramatically in recent years. Desertification across the north of Borno state has, over the last decade, destroyed farmland and sparked an exodus to the city. The academic Mohammed Kabir Isa of Ahmadu Bello University Zaria says: "When they come to the city in search of a livelihood, the bubble bursts, and they realise there's nothing there. That's when they become easy prey for militant organisations."

By the end of 2008, the group was operating like a state within a state; it had its own institutions, including a shura council to make decisions and a religious police force to enforce discipline. It had a rudimentary welfare system, offered jobs working the land it had acquired in Bauchi and even gave microfinance loans to members to start their own projects. Many used the money to buy motorcycles and worked as *achaba* drivers. The group also arranged marriages between members, which many of the poorest could not afford in

2 **to crush** to defeat, to overcome – 2 **self-imposed** decided by oneself – 11 **incarnation** form – 14 **desertification** process by which an area becomes desert – 22 **shura council** (in Islam) consultative council

normal life. Rather than sticking out as rebels, Yusuf and his followers could blend in with ordinary people.

Yusuf was also comfortable moving between the different layers of Maiduguri society. The city has always been an important trading post for dealers in goods of all kinds – legal and otherwise. Its proximity to the borders of three countries – Cameroon, Chad, Niger – makes it an ideal hub for speculation in commodities such as fertiliser, kerosene, diesel and petrol. Maiduguri's trading elite have made a lot of money. Some of them gravitated to Yusuf's Salafist group in the belief that they should atone for their prosperity.

The Ibn Taymiyyah mosque had been allowed to function thanks to a deal that Yusuf had struck with the government. The agreement between the state deputy governor and Yusuf had been brokered in Saudi Arabia by a leading Salafist sheikh. Yusuf promised that he had nothing to do with the separatist group in Kanamma and would never again preach violent jihad. But in the following years, he ignored this pledge and was picked up by the security services several times, only to be swiftly released. The journalist who first reported on Yusuf's sect believes that – at least at this early stage – its leader enjoyed high-level backing from the governor of Borno, Ali Modu Sherif.

Ahmed Salkida, a reporter for the Daily Trust, one of the few Nigerian papers that focus on the north, wrote extensively about the group in the years before 2009. He says that despite his professed loathing of politics, Yusuf made alliances and found common ground with Sherif. Both men had much to gain from cooperation. Yusuf wanted the guarantees of a stronger sharia, a commitment to a strict line on God's divine law; Sherif wanted to be re-elected. Sherif denies any such arrangement or involvement with the sect.

---

10 **to atone** *wiedergutmachen* – 17 **pledge** promise

In public, the two men had an antagonistic relationship. Yusuf had called Sherif an "infidel" and demanded his death. Sherif, however, knew that it would have been unwise to fight Yusuf. Instead, he courted him, providing a lucrative position in the state religious affairs ministry to one of Boko Haram's most zealous members, a man named Buji Foi.

Salkida told me that until the final days before the uprising, Yusuf still believed that a deal could be done with the state, and that Sherif would come around to Boko Haram's uncompromising position. But by that stage Sherif had been backed into a corner. He could no longer protect Yusuf, who was handed over to the police, and quickly executed. Questions still hang over the speed with which Yusuf was dispatched, and who exactly was served by his silencing.

■

After Yusuf's death, his lieutenants went into hiding, but they were sustained by their loyalty to his vision. Under the leadership of Abubakar Shekau, who had been Yusuf's second-in-command, Boko Haram's priority was revenge. The group's first targets were the police, who were attacked at their own checkpoints and robbed of their weapons. Higher-ranking officers were assassinated in their homes, as were local politicians and traditional rulers. After the uprising, the authorities had demanded that traditional leaders help them identify members of Boko Haram, who were then summarily executed, and their property given to the informants as reward. Now the group came back to murder those who had betrayed them, robbing them of what they called the "spoils of war" – wealth that belonged to the jihadi fighters.

---

4 **to court** to try to win sb's support by paying them special attention – 5 **zealous** [ˈzeləs] passionate, fanatic – 13 **to dispatch** *here*: to kill

In June 2011, under cover of darkness, Mohammed Manga, a 35-year-old commercial driver, set out from a camp near Maiduguri for the capital. In his car was an explosive device prepared by either al-Qaida in the Islamic Mahgreb, which was then in camps in the Sahara, or al-Shabaab in Somalia. He drove into the police headquarters, past the sentries and up to the front door, in the middle of a crowd. When he detonated the bomb, five were killed and more than 100 injured.

A spokesman for Boko Haram said that Manga had left his widow and five children a considerable inheritance. A photograph sent to journalists showed him smiling and waving as he got into the car, holding an AK-47. "He was calm and never showed fear," the group's spokesman told Salkida. He added that everyone was envious of Manga, "wishing it was their chance to act and gain entry into paradise".

Boko Haram followed up this mission a few weeks later, in August 2011, by detonating a car packed with explosives in the driveway of the United Nations building in Abuja. At least 21 people were killed and scores wounded.

The group unleashed a bombing campaign in Maiduguri, Jos, Kaduna and the capital, and devastating coordinated strikes against the security services in Kano. It attacked churches, universities and schools, bus stations and markets, killing thousands. Within a few years, between 2011 and 2014, Boko Haram had gone from the tattered remnants of a radical sect, to a fully fledged terrorist group.

As it grew in power, subsuming whole towns by force, the group attracted more and more followers. Bands of armed robbers joined to exploit the chaos it left behind. Others joined to settle ancient

---

10 **inheritance** things (e.g. money, property) left to sb after another person's death –
25 **tattered remnants** reduced to a few leftovers – 25 **fledged** fully developed

scores against rival ethnic religious groups, mostly over land. Others were grabbed off the streets and forced into service.

■

Zakariyya, the young prisoner I met in 2011, had been coerced into joining Boko Haram. In the office of the Special Armed Robbery Squad in Maiduguri, my colleague, Abdullahi Kaura, and I listened as he finished his account.

As a boy, Zakariyya was brought up by his grandmother. His father was not around while he was growing up, and for a great part of his youth, neither was his mother. After his parents divorced, she had married a man who wanted nothing to do with him. After some time, Zakariyya said, his mother returned. She came back with some money, but when that ran out, the family did not have enough for him to continue to attend school. His mother had other, younger, children to care for. He left school with no qualifications and went out hawking. Selling shoes and phone accessories, he was able to take home between 2,000 or 3,000 naira a week (£10). Now 22, he said that he had two wives, and two children. He was struggling to feed his family when the men from Boko Haram offered to pay him to smuggle weapons.

"They promised me 200,000 naira," he said, "but on the first trip they only paid me 70,000 and on the second trip they gave me only 40,000. I was never in favour of their ideology. They threatened me and said that now I knew what they were and who they were, I either did what they wanted or they would kill me. You cannot know their secret and just go. Once you know, you have to be part of them or they would just get rid of you. I was afraid for my life."

---

4 **to coerce** [kəʊˈɜːrs] to force – 16 **to hawk** to sell things informally (on the street)

When he was caught by the police, he told the officers what they wanted to know. "And, now the security forces have arrested me, I have pledged to assist them. Even as it is now, I'm in trouble. If they get me, I'm a dead man."

Zakariyya's voice was very faint. He looked very small.

Boko Haram's violent network across Borno, Adamawa and Yobe went largely unchecked by the military. The group became bolder and began attacking towns in large fighting groups, travelling in convoys of stolen Toyota Hiluxes. Its tactic was to arrive in a town and announce itself at the mosque. After members of the group rounded up everyone they could, they would announce that the young men could either join them, or die. In February 2014, 59 young boys were lined up outside their school dormitory and murdered, their bodies thrown on a fire.

In March 2014 Boko Haram attacked the Giwa barracks in Maiduguri. In a video, men can be seen advancing on the military base, in the suburbs of a state capital under emergency rule. The fighters, many of whom are little more than boys, made almost no attempt to seek cover during their advance. When they broke in, they freed 800 people from the cells. Among the prisoners were people who were not members of Boko Haram before they had been picked up by the military. These people now faced a choice: they could not stay in prison, as they would surely die there. If they left and struck out on their own they risked being recaptured. Or they could leave with the group who had just liberated them.

The fate that met those who did not go with Boko Haram was discovered by Amnesty International: 645 people who refused to join the militants were rounded up and executed, then dumped in a mass grave. For many, like Zakariyya, it must have seemed that their destiny was to join Boko Haram or die.

After our encounter with Zakariyya, my colleague and I stood outside the police station. We were both badly shaken. "They're going to kill that boy aren't they?" I asked.

Kaura nodded.

(This article is adapted from Eat the Heart of the Infidel by Andrew Walker and published by Hurst, London.)

© Andrew Walker

Text 2: My Lord, Tell Me Where to Keep Your Bribe

by Niyi Osundare (2016)

In his remarkable poem "My Lord, Tell Me Where to Keep Your Bribe"
the renowned Nigerian poet, dramatist and literary critic Niyi
Osundare addresses one of Nigeria's most severe and persistent
problems. Corruption has been rife in all areas of Nigerian society for
many decades.

Osundare was born in 1947 and educated in Nigeria, England and
Canada. He is the holder of numerous literary awards and has taught
literature at several universities. Niyi Osundare has always been a
passionate champion of free speech and has refused to remain silent
on important matters, even if this has proved inconvenient for the
government. Due to his criticism and artistic activism against the
Nigerian dictatorship in the 1990s he "preferred" to leave his home
country in 1997 and became Professor of English at the University of
New Orleans.

MY LORD, TELL ME WHERE
TO KEEP YOUR BRIBE

1

My Lord
Please tell me where to keep your bribe
Do I drop it in your venerable chambers
    Or carry the heavy booty to your immaculate mansion

Shall I bury it in the capacious water tank
    In your well laundered backyard
Or will it breathe better in the septic tank
    Since money can deodorize the smelliest crime

Shall I haul it up the attic
    Between the ceiling and your lofty roof
Or shall I conjure the walls to open up
    And swallow this sudden bounty from your honest labour

---

5 **bribe** money offered to sb so they will do sth for you – 6 v**enerable** respected,
honoured – 7 **booty** stolen things – 7 **immaculate mansion** huge, perfectly kept house –
8 **capacious** big – 10 **septic tank** *Klärgrube* – 14 **to conjure** *here*: to call upon, to ask –
15 **bounty** gift, reward

Shall I give a billion to each of your paramours
　　The black, the light, the Fanta-yellow
They will surely know how to keep the loot
　　In places too remote for the sniffing dog

5　Or shall I use the particulars
　　Of your anonymous maidservants and manservants
With their names on overflowing bank accounts
　　While they, the bearers, are starving like ownerless dogs

Shall I haul it all to your village
10　In the valley behind seven mountains
Where potholes swallow up the hugest jeep
　　And Penury leaves a scar on every house

My Lord
　　It will take the fastest machine
15 Many, many days to count this booty; and lucky bank bosses
　　May help themselves to a fraction of the loot

My Lord
　　Tell me where to keep your bribe

---

1 **paramour** (*archaic*) lover − 3 **loot** (*inf*) money − 11 **pothole** deep hole in a street or road −
12 **penury** extreme poverty

2

My Lord
Tell me where to keep your bribe

The "last hope of the common man"
5   Has become the last bastion of the criminally rich
A terrible plague bestrides the land
    Besieged by rapacious judges and venal lawyers

Behind the antiquated wig
    And the slavish glove
10   The penguin gown and the obfuscating jargon
    Is a rot and riot whose stench is choking the land

Behind the rituals and roted rigmaroles
    Old antics connive with new tricks
Behind the prim-and-proper costumes of masquerades
15   Corruption stands, naked, in its insolent impunity

---

5 **bastion** protection, defence – 7 **rapacious** greedy, wanting more (money) – 7 **venal** corrupt – 8 **wig** a covering for the head made of hair – 10 **obfuscating** deliberately confusing – 12 **roted rigmarole** sth that is carried out in the same complicated way over and over again – 13 **to connive** *gemeinsame Sache machen* – 14 **prim-and-proper** behaving in a correct and (socially) acceptable way – 15 **impunity** freedom from punishment

For sale to the highest bidder
   Interlocutory and perpetual injunctions
Opulent criminals shop for pliant judges:
   Protect the criminal, enshrine the crime

5   And *Election Petition Tribunals*
   Ah, bless those goldmines and bottomless booties!
Scoundrel vote-riggers romp to electoral victory
   All hail our buyable Bench and conniving Bar

A million dollars in Their Lordship's bedroom
10   A million euros in the parlor closet
Countless naira beneath the kitchen sink
   Our courts are fast running out of *Ghana-must-go's*

The "Temple of Justice"
   Is broken in every brick
15   The roof is roundly perforated
   By termites of graft

---

2 **interlocutory injunction** (*law*) *einstweilige Verfügung* – 2 **perpetual** permanent – 3 **pliant** easily influenced – 5 **Election Petition Tribunal** court that deals with challenges to the result of an election – 7 **vote-rigger** person who manipulates votes – 12 **Ghana-must-go** large, extremely tough bag used for carrying heavy cash in Nigeria – 15 **perforated** containing holes – 16 **graft** (*pol*) using power to obtain money dishonestly

3

My Lord
    Tell me where to keep your bribe

Judges doze in the courtroom
    Having spent all night, counting money and various "gifts"
And the Chief Justice looks on with tired eyes
    As Corruption usurps his gavel.

Crime pays in this country
    Corruption has its handsome rewards
Just one judgement sold to the richest bidder
    Will catapult Judge & Lawyer to the Billionaires' Club

The Law, they say, is an ass
    Sometimes fast, sometimes slow
But the Law in Nigeria is a vulture
    Fat on the cash-and-carry carrion of murdered Conscience

Won gb'ebi f'alare
    Won gb'are f'elebi
They kill our trust in the common good
    These Monsters of Mammon in their garish gowns

---

7 **to usurp** to use sth without the right to do so – 7 **gavel** *Richterhammer* – 10 **bidder**
person who makes an offer for sth – 14 **vulture** *Geier* – 15 **carrion** dead and rotten
flesh – 16 **Won gb'ebi f'alare** They declare the innocent guilty – 17 **Won gb'are f'elebi** They
pronounce the guilty innocent – 19 **garish** very bright

Unhappy the land
　Where jobbers are judges
Where Impunity walks the streets
　Like a large, invincible Demon

Come Sunday, they troop to the church
　Friday, they mouth their mantra in pious mosques
But they pervert Justice all week long
　And dig us deeper into the hellish hole

Our country is a huge corpse
　With milling maggots on its wretched hulk
They prey every day, they prey every night
　For the endless decomposition of our common soul

My Most Honourable Lord
　Just tell me where to keep your bribe.

© Niyi Osundare

---

6 **pious** very religious and moral – 10 **maggot** *Made* – 10 **hulk** ruined remains

Text 3: The Thing Around Your Neck

by Chimamanda Ngozi Adichie (2009)

Novelist Chimamanda Ngozi Adichie is one of Nigeria's most successful writers. The Times Literary Supplement has written of her that she is one of a new generation of anglophone authors "attracting a new generation of readers to African literature." One of five children she grew up in Nigeria under the influence of post-colonialism before moving to America to study. She now splits her time between Nigeria and the US.

In her short story "The thing around her neck" Ngozi Adichie describes the life of a young woman called Akunna after she has gained an American visa and goes to live with her uncle and aunt in New England. However, Akunna finds that life away from the comforting familiarity of place and culture may perhaps not be the American Dream many hope for. Torn between her new American way of life and her old life in Nigeria, Akunna must decide where she belongs.

You thought everybody in America had a car and a gun; your uncles and aunts and cousins thought so, too. Right after you won the American visa lottery, they told you: In a month, you will have a big car. Soon, a big house. But don't buy a gun like those Americans.

They trooped into the room in Lagos where you lived with your father and mother and three siblings, leaning against the unpainted walls because there weren't enough chairs to go round, to say goodbye in loud voices and tell you with lowered voices what they wanted you to send them. In comparison to the big car and house (and possibly gun), the things they wanted were minor—handbags and shoes and perfumes and clothes. You said okay, no problem.

Your uncle in America, who had put in the names of all your family members for the American visa lottery, said you could live with him until you got on your feet. He picked you up at the airport and bought you a big hot dog with yellow mustard that nauseated you. Introduction to America, he said with a laugh. He lived in a small white town in Maine, in a thirty-year-old house by a lake. He told you that the company he worked for had offered him a few thousand more than the average salary plus stock options because they were desperately trying to look diverse. They included a photo of him in every brochure, even those that had nothing to do with his unit. He laughed and said the job was good, was worth living in an all-white town even though his wife had to drive an hour to find a hair salon that did black hair. The trick was to understand America, to know that America was give-and-take. You gave up a lot but you gained a lot, too.

He showed you how to apply for a cashier job in the gas station on Main Street and he enrolled you in a community college, where the girls had thick thighs and wore bright-red nail polish, and self-

---

5 **to troop** to stream, to gather – 15 **to nauseate** to make sb feel sick – 29 **self-tanner** *Selbstbräunungscreme*

tanner that made them look orange. They asked where you learned to speak English and if you had real houses back in Africa and if you'd seen a car before you came to America. They gawped at your hair. Does it stand up or fall down when you take out the braids? They wanted to know. All of it stands up? How? Why? Do you use a comb? You smiled tightly when they asked those questions. Your uncle told you to expect it; a mixture of ignorance and arrogance, he called it. Then he told you how the neighbors said, a few months after he moved into his house, that the squirrels had started to disappear. They had heard that Africans ate all kinds of wild animals.

You laughed with your uncle and you felt at home in his house; his wife called you *nwanne*, sister, and his two school-age children called you Aunty. They spoke Igbo and ate *garri* for lunch and it was like home. Until your uncle came into the cramped basement where you slept with old boxes and cartons and pulled you forcefully to him, squeezing your buttocks, moaning. He wasn't really your uncle; he was actually a brother of your father's sister's husband, not related by blood. After you pushed him away, he sat on your bed— it was his house, after all—and smiled and said you were no longer a child at twentytwo. If you let him, he would do many things for you. Smart women did it all the time. How did you think those women back home in Lagos with well-paying jobs made it? Even women in New York City?

You locked yourself in the bathroom until he went back upstairs, and the next morning, you left, walking the long windy road, smelling the baby fish in the lake. You saw him drive past—he had always dropped you off at Main Street—and he didn't honk. You wondered what he would tell his wife, why you had left. And you remembered what he said, that America was give-and-take.

---

3 **to gawp** (*inf*) to stare – 4 **braid** three pieces of hair twisted together – 9 **squirrel** [ˈskwɜrəl] *Eichhörnchen* – 13 **Igbo** [ˈiːboʊ] language of the Igbo people in southeastern Nigeria – 13 **garri** Nigerian dish made of manioc – 27 **to honk** to blow a car horn

You ended up in Connecticut, in another little town, because it was the last stop of the Greyhound bus you got on. You walked into the restaurant with the bright, clean awning and said you would work for two dollars less than the other waitresses. The manager, Juan, had inky-black hair and smiled to show a gold tooth. He said he had never had a Nigerian employee but all immigrants worked hard. He knew, he'd been there. He'd pay you a dollar less, but under the table; he didn't like all the taxes they were making him pay.

You could not afford to go to school, because now you paid rent for the tiny room with the stained carpet. Besides, the small Connecticut town didn't have a community college and credits at the state university cost too much. So you went to the public library, you looked up course syllabi on school Web sites and read some of the books. Sometimes you sat on the lumpy mattress of your twin bed and thought about home—your aunts who hawked dried fish and plantains, cajoling customers to buy and then shouting insults when they didn't; your uncles who drank local gin and crammed their families and lives into single rooms; your friends who had come out to say goodbye before you left, to rejoice because you won the American visa lottery, to confess their envy; your parents who often held hands as they walked to church on Sunday mornings, the neighbors from the next room laughing and teasing them; your father who brought back his boss's old newspapers from work and made your brothers read them; your mother whose salary was barely enough to pay your brothers' school fees at the secondary school where teachers gave an A when someone slipped them a brown envelope.

---

3 **awning** *Markise, Vordach* – 10 **stained** dirty – 13 **syllabus** [ˈsɪləbəs] (*pl* syllabi) curriculum (*Studienprogramm*) – 15 **to hawk** to sell – 16 **plantain** type of green banana that is cooked and eaten as a vegetable – 16 **to cajole sb** [kəˈdʒoʊl] to persuade sb to do sth

You had never needed to pay for an A, never slipped a brown envelope to a teacher in secondary school. Still, you chose long brown envelopes to send half your month's earnings to your parents at the address of the parastatal where your mother was a cleaner; you always used the dollar notes that Juan gave you because those were crisp, unlike the tips. Every month. You wrapped the money carefully in white paper but you didn't write a letter. There was nothing to write about.

In later weeks, though, you wanted to write because you had stories to tell. You wanted to write about the surprising openness of people in America, how eagerly they told you about their mother fighting cancer, about their sister-in-law's preemie, the kinds of things that one should hide or should reveal only to the family members who wished them well. You wanted to write about the way people left so much food on their plates and crumpled a few dollar bills down, as though it was an offering, expiation for the wasted food. You wanted to write about the child who started to cry and pull at her blond hair and push the menus off the table and instead of the parents making her shut up, they pleaded with her, a child of perhaps five years old, and then they all got up and left. You wanted to write about the rich people who wore shabby clothes and tattered sneakers, who looked like the night watchmen in front of the large compounds in Lagos. You wanted to write that rich Americans were thin and poor Americans were fat and that many did not have a big house and car; you still were not sure about the guns, though, because they might have them inside their pockets.

It wasn't just to your parents you wanted to write, it was also to your friends, and cousins and aunts and uncles. But you could never

---

4 **parastatal** state-owned organization − 12 **preemie** (*sl*) baby born too early −
16 **expiation** (*form*) *Sühne, Buße* − 21 **tattered** in poor condition, falling to pieces

afford enough perfumes and clothes and handbags and shoes to go around and still pay your rent on what you earned at the waitressing job, so you wrote nobody.

Nobody knew where you were, because you told no one. Sometimes you felt invisible and tried to walk through your room wall into the hallway, and when you bumped into the wall, it left bruises on your arms. Once, Juan asked if you had a man that hit you because he would take care of him and you laughed a mysterious laugh.

At night, something would wrap itself around your neck, something that very nearly choked you before you fell asleep.

Many people at the restaurant asked when you had come from Jamaica, because they thought that every black person with a foreign accent was Jamaican. Or some who guessed that you were African told you that they loved elephants and wanted to go on a safari.

So when he asked you, in the dimness of the restaurant after you recited the daily specials, what African country you were from, you said Nigeria and expected him to say that he had donated money to fight AIDS in Botswana. But he asked if you were Yoruba or Igbo, because you didn't have a Fulani face. You were surprised—you thought he must be a professor of anthropology at the state university, a little young in his late twenties or so, but who was to say? Igbo, you said. He asked your name and said Akunna was pretty. He did not ask what it meant, fortunately, because you were sick of how people said, " 'Father's Wealth'? You mean, like, your father will actually sell you to a husband?"

---

11 **to choke** to prevent sb from breathing – 16 **dimness** darkness – 20 **Fulani** one of the largest ethnic groups in West Africa

He told you he had been to Ghana and Uganda and Tanzania, loved the poetry of Okot p'Bitek and the novels of Amos Tutuola and had read a lot about sub-Saharan African countries, their histories, their complexities. You wanted to feel disdain, to show it as you brought his order, because white people who liked Africa too much and those who liked Africa too little were the same—condescending. But he didn't shake his head in the superior way that Professor Cobbledick back in the Maine community college did during a class discussion on decolonization in Africa. He didn't have that expression of Professor Cobbledick's, that expression of a person who thought himself better than the people he knew about. He came in the next day and sat at the same table and when you asked if the chicken was okay, he asked if you had grown up in Lagos. He came in the third day and began talking before he ordered, about how he had visited Bombay and now wanted to visit Lagos, to see how real people lived, like in the shantytowns, because he never did any of the silly tourist stuff when he was abroad. He talked and talked and you had to tell him it was against restaurant policy. He brushed your hand when you set the glass of water down. The fourth day, when you saw him arrive, you told Juan you didn't want that table anymore. After your shift that night, he was waiting outside, earphones stuck in his ears, asking you to go out with him because your name rhymed with *hakuna matata* and *The Lion King* was the only maudlin movie he'd ever liked. You didn't know what *The Lion King* was. You looked at him in the bright light and noticed that his eyes were the color of extra-virgin olive oil, a greenish gold. Extra-virgin olive oil was the only thing you loved, truly loved, in America.

---

2 **Okot p'Bitek** (1931–1982) Ugandan poet – 2 **Amos Tutuola** (1920–1997) Nigerian writer whose books were partly based on Yoruba folktales. – 4 **disdain** *Missachtung, Geringschätzung* – 7 **condescending** *herablassend* – 24 **maudlin** very sentimental

He was a senior at the state university. He told you how old he was and you asked why he had not graduated yet. This was America, after all, it was not like back home, where universities closed so often that people added three years to their normal course of study and lecturers went on strike after strike and still were not paid. He said he had taken a couple of years off to discover himself and travel, mostly to Africa and Asia. You asked him where he ended up finding himself and he laughed. You did not laugh. You did not know that people could simply choose not to go to school, that people could dictate to life. You were used to accepting what life gave, writing down what life dictated.

You said no the following four days to going out with him, because you were uncomfortable with the way he looked at your face, that intense, consuming way he looked at your face that made you say goodbye to him but also made you reluctant to walk away. And then, the fifth night, you panicked when he was not standing at the door after your shift. You prayed for the first time in a long time and when he came up behind you and said hey, you said yes, you would go out with him, even before he asked. You were scared he would not ask again.

The next day, he took you to dinner at Chang's and your fortune cookie had two strips of paper. Both of them were blank.

You knew you had become comfortable when you told him that you watched *Jeopardy* on the restaurant TV and that you rooted for the following, in this order: women of color, black men, and white women, before, finally, white men—which meant you never rooted for white men. He laughed and told you he was used to not being rooted for, his mother taught women's studies.

---

15 reluctant unwilling, not wanting to

And you knew you had become close when you told him that your father was really not a schoolteacher in Lagos, that he was a junior driver for a construction company. And you told him about that day in Lagos traffic in the rickety Peugeot 504 your father drove; it was raining and your seat was wet because of the rust-eaten hole in the roof. The traffic was heavy, the traffic was always heavy in Lagos, and when it rained it was chaos. The roads became muddy ponds and cars got stuck and some of your cousins went out and made some money pushing the cars out. The rain, the swampiness, you thought, made your father step on the brakes too late that day. You heard the bump before you felt it. The car your father rammed into was wide, foreign, and dark green, with golden headlights like the eyes of a leopard. Your father started to cry and beg even before he got out of the car and laid himself flat on the road, causing much blowing of horns. Sorry sir, sorry sir, he chanted. If you sell me and my family, you cannot buy even one tire on your car. Sorry sir.

The Big Man seated at the back did not come out, but his driver did, examining the damage, looking at your father's sprawled form from the corner of his eye as though the pleading was like pornography, a performance he was ashamed to admit he enjoyed. At last he let your father go. Waved him away. The other cars' horns blew and drivers cursed. When your father came back into the car, you refused to look at him because he was just like the pigs that wallowed in the marshes around the market. Your father looked like *nsi*. Shit.

After you told him this, he pursed his lips and held your hand and said he understood how you felt. You shook your hand free, suddenly annoyed, because he thought the world was, or ought to be, full of people like him. You told him there was nothing to understand, it was just the way it was.

---

4 **rickety** about to break, falling apart – 9 **swamp** [swɑːmp] *Feuchtgebiet* – 18 **to sprawl** [sprɑːl] to sit or lie spread out – 24 **marsh** wet, muddy area of land

He found the African store in the Hartford yellow pages and drove you there. Because of the way he walked around with familiarity, tilting the bottle of palm wine to see how much sediment it had, the Ghanaian store owner asked him if he was African, like the white Kenyans or South Africans, and he said yes, but he'd been in America for a long time. He looked pleased that the store owner had believed him. You cooked that evening with the things you had bought, and after he ate *garri* and *onugbu* soup, he threw up in your sink. You didn't mind, though, because now you would be able to cook *onugbu* soup with meat.

He didn't eat meat because he thought it was wrong the way they killed animals; he said they released fear toxins into the animals and the fear toxins made people paranoid. Back home, the meat pieces you ate, when there was meat, were the size of half your finger. But you did not tell him that. You did not tell him either that the *dawadawa* cubes your mother cooked everything with, because curry and thyme were too expensive, had MSG, *were* MSG. He said MSG caused cancer, it was the reason he liked Chang's; Chang didn't cook with MSG.

Once, at Chang's, he told the waiter he had recently visited Shanghai, that he spoke some Mandarin. The waiter warmed up and told him what soup was best and then asked him, "You have girlfriend in Shanghai now?" And he smiled and said nothing.

You lost your appetite, the region deep in your chest felt clogged. That night, you didn't moan when he was inside you, you bit your lips and pretended that you didn't come because you knew he would worry. Later you told him why you were upset, that even though you went to Chang's so often together, even though you had kissed

---

3 **palm wine** alcoholic beverage made from the sap of palm trees – 3 **sediment** *Bodensatz* – 8 **onugbu soup** popular Igbo soup with bitter leaf spinach – 12 **toxin** poison – 16 **dawadawa** type of stock cube (*Brühwürfel*) used to spice foods – 17 **thyme** *Thymian* – 17 **MSG** (*abbr* of monosodium glutamate) *Glutamat* – 24 **clogged** blocked

just before the menus came, the Chinese man had assumed you could not possibly be his girlfriend, and he had smiled and said nothing. Before he apologized, he gazed at you blankly and you knew that he did not understand.

He bought you presents and when you objected about the cost, he said his grandfather in Boston had been wealthy but hastily added that the old man had given a lot away and so the trust fund he had wasn't huge. His presents mystified you. A fist-size glass ball that you shook to watch a tiny, shapely doll in pink spin around. A shiny rock whose surface took on the color of whatever touched it. An expensive scarf hand-painted in Mexico. Finally you told him, your voice stretched in irony, that in your life presents were always useful. The rock, for instance, would work if you could grind things with it. He laughed long and hard but you did not laugh. You realized that in his life, he could buy presents that were just presents and nothing else, nothing useful. When he started to buy you shoes and clothes and books, you asked him not to, you didn't want any presents at all. He bought them anyway and you kept them for your cousins and uncles and aunts, for when you would one day be able to visit home, even though you did not know how you could ever afford a ticket and your rent. He said he really wanted to see Nigeria and he could pay for you both to go. You did not want him to pay for you to visit home. You did not want him to go to Nigeria, to add it to the list of countries where he went to gawk at the lives of poor people who could never gawk back at his life. You told him this on a sunny day, when he took you to see Long Island Sound, and the two of you argued, your voices raised as you walked along the calm water. He said you were wrong to call him self-righteous. You said

---

8 **to mystify** to confuse – 28 **self-righteous** believing oneself to be superior or right

he was wrong to call only the poor Indians in Bombay the real Indians. Did it mean he wasn't a real American, since he was not like the poor fat people you and he had seen in Hartford? He hurried ahead of you, his upper body bare and pale, his flip-flops raising bits of sand, but then he came back and held out his hand for yours. You made up and made love and ran your hands through each other's hair, his soft and yellow like the swinging tassels of growing corn, yours dark and bouncy like the filling of a pillow. He had got too much sun and his skin turned the color of a ripe water melon and you kissed his back before you rubbed lotion on it.

The thing that wrapped itself around your neck, that nearly choked you before you fell asleep, started to loosen, to let go.

You knew by people's reactions that you two were abnormal—the way the nasty ones were too nasty and the nice ones too nice. The old white men and women who muttered and glared at him, the black men who shook their heads at you, the black women whose pitying eyes bemoaned your lack of self-esteem, your self-loathing. Or the black women who smiled swift solidarity smiles; the black men who tried too hard to forgive you, saying a too-obvious hi to him; the white men and women who said "What a good-looking pair" too brightly, too loudly, as though to prove their own open-mindedness to themselves.

But his parents were different; they almost made you think it was all normal. His mother told you that he had never brought a girl to meet them, except for his high school prom date, and he grinned stiffly and held your hand. The tablecloth shielded your clasped hands. He squeezed your hand and you squeezed back and wondered

---

7 **tassel** *Quaste, Troddel* – 8 **bouncy** *here: elastisch* – 17 **to bemoan** [bɪˈməʊn] (*form*) to express sadness or dissatisfaction

why he was so stiff, why his extra-virginolive-oil-colored eyes darkened as he spoke to his parents. His mother was delighted when she asked if you'd read Nawal el Saadawi and you said yes. His father asked how similar Indian food was to Nigerian food and teased you about paying when the check came. You looked at them and felt grateful that they did not examine you like an exotic trophy, an ivory tusk.

Afterwards, he told you about his issues with his parents, how they portioned out love like a birthday cake, how they would give him a bigger slice if only he'd agree to go to law school. You wanted to sympathize. But instead you were angry.

You were angrier when he told you he had refused to go up to Canada with them for a week or two, to their summer cottage in the Quebec countryside. They had even asked him to bring you. He showed you pictures of the cottage and you wondered why it was called a cottage because the buildings that big around your neighborhood back home were banks and churches. You dropped a glass and it shattered on the hardwood of his apartment floor and he asked what was wrong and you said nothing, although you thought a lot was wrong. Later, in the shower, you started to cry. You watched the water dilute your tears and you didn't know why you were crying.

You wrote home finally. A short letter to your parents, slipped in between the crisp dollar bills, and you included your address. You got a reply only days later, by courier. Your mother wrote the letter herself; you knew from the spidery penmanship, from the misspelled words.

---

3 **Nawal el Saadawi** (*1931) Egyptian author and advocate of women's rights – 6 **ivory tusk** long curved tooth from an elephant – 21 **to dilute** to make weaker, reduce the effect of sth – 26 **penmanship** handwriting

Your father was dead; he had slumped over the steering wheel of his company car. Five months now, she wrote. They had used some of the money you sent to give him a good funeral: They killed a goat for the guests and buried him in a good coffin. You curled up in bed, pressed your knees to your chest, and tried to remember what you had been doing when your father died, what you had been doing for all the months when he was already dead. Perhaps your father died on the day your whole body had been covered in goosebumps, hard as uncooked rice, that you could not explain, Juan teasing you about taking over from the chef so that the heat in the kitchen would warm you up. Perhaps your father died on one of the days you took a drive to Mystic or watched a play in Manchester or had dinner at Chang's.

He held you while you cried, smoothed your hair, and offered to buy your ticket, to go with you to see your family. You said no, you needed to go alone. He asked if you would come back and you reminded him that you had a green card and you would lose it if you did not come back in one year. He said you knew what he meant, would you come back, come back?

You turned away and said nothing, and when he drove you to the airport, you hugged him tight for a long, long moment, and then you let go.

© Chimamanda Ngozi Adichie

---

8 **goosebumps** *Gänsehaut*

Text 4: American Dream

by Nonyelum Ekwempu (Red Rock Review, 2016)

Nonyelum Ekwempu is a Nigerian writer and visual artist who grew up both in the bustling city of Lagos and smaller villages in the south
5 *of the country. Her art is inspired by jazz, the colours and vibrancy of African culture and the African immigrant experience. She is currently studying medicine in Chicago.*

Ekwempu's short story "American Dream" was shortlisted for the Caine Prize in 2018, awarded every year to the best original short story
10 *by an African writer. For many Nigerians the chance to live the American Dream, of being part of America's way of life and escaping their old, less tolerable lives would be a dream come true. In the story the 11-year-old protagonist and narrator Ade tells the reader of his destiny, as proclaimed by the pastor in his church: to be an "Americanah",*
15 *someone destined to emigrate to America and climb up the social ladder of success. Growing up in desperate poverty in the slums of Lagos, having already given up everything once before, Ade juggles his duty to support his mother with dreaming of how to fulfill his destiny.*

I was eleven when Prophet Ajanaku announced in front of the whole church that I was destined to live in America.

"This one is an Americanah," he'd said. "His enemies have seen this and they are not happy. That's why they want to take him before his time. Church let us pray."

He sprinkled holy water on my head and rang his bell in circles seven times. In the middle of the prayer, I looked up at my mother and noticed that happiness had suddenly descended on her. I had been sick with malaria for seven days, and for those seven days she'd worn sadness as clothes. Her sadness turned into panic. Panic turned to anguish when she found me foaming at the mouth and shaking without control. But as the prophet blessed me, the corners of her mouth were turned up and her face glowed with optimism.

For many years after that day, my mother would clutch tightly to those few words about my future and they would lift and soothe her soul as she struggled to build a new life without my father. I remember that day in church clearly because it was also the one year anniversary of my father's death, and exactly ten months since we had moved from our house in Surulere to our new home in Makoko, a sprawling slum on the Lagos lagoon. There were no official numbers for the population of the slum, but people said that between 85,000 and 250,000 people lived in the tightly packed shanty houses that hovered precariously over stagnant waters on uneven wooden stilts.

A lot changed in the year after my father's death, but the move to Makoko was the biggest change for me. A week after we'd moved into our new home, I noticed a cluster of ringworm develop on the left side of my neck. Then without warning, I woke up one morning

---

11 **anguish** extreme unhappiness – 11 **to foam** *schäumen* – 20 **sprawling** covering a big area – 23 **stagnant** not moving and smelling unpleasant – 27 **ringworm** *Ringelflechte (Hautkrankheit)*

to find that it had spread all over my body, including my scalp. My mother shaved my head and kept it shaved for the months that the ringworm lingered. On my first day at my new school, I felt embarrassed walking into my crowded classroom. I imagined that the other children would stare and point at the new boy with no hair and ringworm colonies running up and down his arms and legs. But that didn't happen. And I quickly realized that having ringworm or some sort of skin disease was not an oddity at the school.

Life in Makoko revolved around the lagoon. There was no clay soil, no concrete, and no dirt roads to stand on, to tumble in cartwheels on, or to play soccer. All of that was no longer part of my life. And clay soil and open dirt roads now felt so distant, as if they had only been a figment of my imagination. The other children in Makoko didn't seem to mind that they didn't have these things. Most of them were born here and had learned to swim before they could walk. Their lives followed a predictable pattern. They went to school if their parents decided on it. They learned to swim and paddle wooden canoes with a straight bamboo stick. The boys learned how to build the narrow, wooden crafts and how to fish. The girls learned how to smoke the fish and how to sell it along with other goods. This was their way of life and anything different would be so foreign that it would require some time to adjust.

On some evenings, some of the boys stopped by my house in their canoes and we paddled out into the open lagoon, away from the other houses, the barking dogs, the women selling goods from the ribbed bottoms of their canoes, and the chaos of our organic, unplanned neighborhood. We fished and watched cars and buses

---

8 **oddity** unusual thing or situation – 10 **clay soil** *Lehmboden* – 11 **concrete** stonelike grey material used to build things – 14 **figment** invention – 21 **to smoke** *here: räuchern* – 27 **ribbed** *gerippt*

crawl through traffic on the Third Mainland Bridge in the distance. The boys taught me how to cast a net and how to swim.

When I felt confident in my swimming skills, I called my mother and my two younger sisters out to the little porch in front of our house and I leaped off the peeling wooden rail into the brownish-black water below. They jumped in excitement as they watched me alternate between the breaststroke, the backstroke and the front crawl. My sisters asked me to teach them to swim and we started lessons right away. My mother kept a watchful eye from above, in case she needed to scream for help. She didn't know how to swim, and I could tell that she was proud of me, just like she was whenever I brought fish home from my outings with the boys. After a while, she got tired of watching and she went inside.

Our house was a square room with two windows on the same side as our door. We had tiptoed around the room for the first two weeks after we moved in, afraid that the thin wood sheets that suspended us over the waste and sewage-filled lagoon would give in under our weight. My mother had placed a queen-sized mattress that took up half the space of the room on the wall directly across from the door and windows. In a corner near one of the windows, she kept a small kerosene stove that always ran out midway through her cooking. Sometimes she'd ask me to go and beg Iya Tubosun, who lived next door, for more.

Iya Tubosun was my mother's closest friend in the neighborhood, and she always seemed willing to give my mother whatever she asked for—cooking seasoning, toothpaste, kerosene, calamine lotion for Tosin's measles, detergent. When we first moved in, she lent us one of her canoes until my mother saved up enough money to buy her own. On some mornings, she stopped by our house with

---

5 **peeling** with the paint coming off – 15 **to tiptoe** to walk silently on toes – 17 **sewage** waste water and waste from toilets – 26 **calamine lotion** lotion to treat itchiness and skin diseases – 27 **detergent** soap, cleaner

Agege bread and hard boiled eggs that she bought from hawkers who paddled around the neighborhood in their canoes, shouting, "Come and buy *Agege* bread 'o," in Yoruba. Iya Tubosun would hand the food to my mother, and then place her fat hands on my mother's thin waist to twist her hips from side to side, admiring them as if they were new shoes.

"If I thin like you, *ehn*, I for done go international. All these oyinbo men on the Island, na them I go dey sell my market to," she'd say. My mother would laugh shyly, avert her gaze from Iya Tubosun, and pretend to not be flattered.

No one dared to offend Iya Tubosun, a woman who walked with an air of confidence and certainty engendered a sense of assurance and a sliver of fear. Her short, stout build, deep red eyes, and horizontal tribal marks that ran across her puffy cheeks only added to the effect.

She was the type of woman who knew how to make things happen, the kind of woman who couldn't be shortchanged on anything. The first time she knocked on our door, which was on the day we moved in, Tosin, who was three at the time, refused to look at Iya Tubosun's face or to collect the biscuit that Iya Tubosun held out to her. Later that day, Iya Tubosun brought her four children to greet my mother. She ordered her son Jide, who was a year younger than me, to pick me up for school in their canoe every morning. Jide frowned and grumbled something incomprehensible to himself. I'd been surprised that she didn't put Tubosun who was my age in charge of the task. But he didn't seem to mind that the task had been delegated to his younger brother. Before Iya Tubosun left our house that day, she told my mother to let her know if anyone gave us

---

1 **Agege bread** Nigerian bread used to make sandwiches – 3 **Yoruba** language of the Yoruba people, an ethnic group inhabiting western Africa – 8 **oyinbo** Yoruba word for "foreign" or "white" – 12 **to engender** to cause, to create – 17 **to shortchange** to cheat, to treat sb unfairly

trouble as we settled into the neighborhood. I was happy my mother had gained the friendship of a woman whose place in Makoko was unquestioned and firmly rooted.

But their friendship didn't last long. One Saturday morning, I woke up to find my mother and Iya Tubosun trading harsh words, each woman trying to out scream the other. My mother called Iya Tubosun an *ashewo*, a third-class prostitute. The crowd of neighbors and strangers who had gathered to watch the mildly entertaining scuffle looked to Iya Tubosun for a reaction.

Mama Bisi stood between my mother and Iya Tobosun, restraining them from exchanging more than words. When either woman hurled an insult and tightened her wrapper, as if in preparation to get physical, Mama Bisi ran to wrap her body around the woman, shouting, "H'is h'okay. H'is hokay 'o. Let there be peace. Me hi've said my h'own." But then her face would betray her words. She'd glance at the other woman, searching for a response. She yelled to my mother in a moment of unnecessary self-aggrandizement, "H'if to say hi' not here, Iya Tubosun for finish you."

But Iya Tubosun had already won the fight and the crowd. My mother stood in a corner, exhausted and at a loss for words, her hands folded over her flat chest. Tears gathered in her eyes and remained there. She shook her head in the pitiful way she did whenever she thought of my father's death. How swift and unexpected—alive and vibrant in the morning, slight headache in the afternoon, dead before sunset.

My mother had used her best line when she called Iya Tubosun an *ashewo*. But it had failed to have the desired effect she had hoped it would. It didn't sting like hot iron on the skin.

It left her mouth and fell flat at Iya Tubosun's feet.

---

9 **scuffle** fight, brawl – 12 **wrapper** *here*: dressing gown – 17 **self-aggrandizement** *Selbstverherrlichung*

The crowd had not gasped the way they did when Iya Tubosun called my mother a "wretched widow" or when she called me a "prancing ringworm infested beggar." But then again, it was also an open secret that Iya Tubosun was a sex worker. I saw men of all ages and body types either running away shyly from her room or knocking quietly at her door, trying not to attract the unwanted gazes of the jobless neighbors who sat outside and gossiped.

I wanted to go outside and put my arms around my mother's bony shoulders. I wanted to remind her and announce to the familiar and unknown faces that my mother has a son who is destined to live in America, a son who is an Americanah.

If Prophet Ajanaku had said it, then it had to be true. Prophet Ajanaku would not lie. He hears directly from God, he is God's anointed. God reveals himself to him in a way that he does not to other people. That is the reason why the Holy Prophet, as we were ordered to call Prophet Ajanaku in church, is able to see things in the future that other people cannot see.

It is the reason why people fall to the ground when he places his hands on their foreheads. It is the reason why women who visit our church complaining about barrenness come back nine months later carrying new born babies. It is the reason why some church members get new jobs just days after he tells them that they will. It is the reason why people who have all kinds of sicknesses come to our church and later give testimonies of miraculous healings after the Holy Prophet has touched them. Some people are even healed without his touch. One time a crippled woman stood from her wheelchair and started running around the altar after the Holy Prophet's sweat fell upon her by accident. I was in church that day and I saw everything with my own eyes. Prophet Ajanaku was

---

7 **gaze** a long intent look – 14 **anointed** chosen successor – 20 **barrenness** the inability to have babies – 24 **testimony** *here*: evidence, proof

shouting into the microphone as he prayed. He was sweating profusely, as usual, but he did not have the small red towel that he always uses to wipe the sweat from his face and neck. At some point, he ran his index finger across his forehead to wipe away the beads that had formed there. Then he flicked his hands to get rid of the sweat. It flew in the woman's direction, and she was healed.

I did not go outside and let the crowd know what the Holy Prophet had said about me. My mother would have knocked my head with her knuckles if I did. She did not want anyone besides the people who were in church on that day to know what lay in my future. She feared that people would be jealous and that they might try to stop it from happening. I don't know how people are able to do such things. But I know that no one can be trusted, not even your uncles and aunties.

The conditions of people's love are fragile and superficial.

One day they can have your back and then the next they can come after you with a wickedness that will shake you at your core and uproot the anchors of your life.

I learned this after my father died. His brothers and sisters—my uncles and aunties—showed me a part of themselves that I didn't know lay within them all the years my father was alive. Daddy was the first born, and he was also the first to live in Lagos. After he graduated from secondary school, he left his small town to study Mathematics on a full scholarship at the University of Lagos. This was when Nigeria was still "good" as he liked to say.

A sepia picture of daddy smiling proudly in his graduation gown hung on the wall above our television back in Surulere. After he graduated, he got a job in the oil industry, and from his paycheck

---

15 **superficial** only on the surface – 18 **anchor** *here*: sth that provides support and security – 26 **sepia** brown (like old photographs)

he put Uncle Tayo, Uncle Segun, Aunty Titi, and Aunty Fisayo through school.

I was nine when Aunty Fisayo finished up her degree in Mass Communication at Lagos State University. Like my other uncles and aunties, she, too, lived with us while she went to school and after she graduated. She and Aunty Titi shared a room in our four-bedroom bungalow while Uncle Tayo and Uncle Segun lived in the boys' quarters. I enjoyed having all my uncles and aunties around. But Uncle Tayo was my favorite.

Even though he was older than Uncle Segun, Aunty Titi, and Aunty Fisayo, he acted younger. He walked with a bounce like some of the teenaged boys on our street, bending his shoulders, listening to music through his Walkman, and moving his arms with a swagger that made girls listen when he talked to them. He had come to Lagos with dreams of studying Law at the same university that daddy graduated from many years earlier.

His admission letter stated that he had been admitted into the Law program, only for him and dozens of his other freshman classmates to arrive on campus to discover that their offers had been rescinded without any explanations. The university offered them spots in the English and the Theatre Arts departments instead. Uncle Tayo chose to major in English. Five years after graduation, he remained unemployed, or underemployed, I should say, since he was cutting people's hair for a living. If he had any resentment about where his cards had fallen, he didn't show it. Or maybe I wasn't observant enough.

On weekends, he blasted Michael Jackson songs from his radio while he hand-washed his clothes outside in the courtyard. I would sit with him, listening to his stories of how the university had

---

13 **swagger** arrogant, confident manner – 20 **to rescind** to cancel, to take back

changed so much over the last few years, watching his muscles stiffen as he wrung water from the wet clothes. I enjoyed comparing the stories he told of his school to the stories dad told.

Unlike daddy's stories, there were no campus gardens, no
5 exhilarating road trips around the country and other parts of West Africa with other students, and no cheery lecturers in Uncle Tayo's stories. Everything was dark and gloomy—lengthy strikes that stretched four-year degrees to eight years, hungry unpaid lecturers who charged students fees for their final exam results, cultist
10 students who slashed other students' throats with machetes and terrorized the campus. His stories were a reflection of what the country had become since the good days were displaced by successive coups and brutal military regimes.

On some Saturday afternoons, Uncle Tayo took me out. I always
15 looked forward to our outings. We usually went to the bookstores in CMS and bought cheap secondhand books. And then on our way home, he always bought me either a meat pie from Mr. Biggs or an ice cream from the ice cream men who rode around on bicycles. Once, when I was eight, he took me to the Bar beach in Victoria
20 Island. It was a pleasant surprise.

That was the first time I saw the Atlantic Ocean and a horse. I asked Uncle Tayo if I could ride on one of the emaciated animals that took beach visitors on five-minute rides beside the crashing waves. But he didn't have enough money to pay for a ride. Instead,
25 he asked a gaunt-faced handler if I could touch his horse. The man shouted at us in Hausa and threatened to hit us with the whip he used on the horses. We ran away disappointed.

---

5 **exhilarating** [eg'zɪləreɪtɪŋ] stimulating, exciting – 9 **cult** small religious group with strange practices and rituals – 16 **CMS** (*abbr of* Christian Missionary Society) location in Lagos – 22 **emaciated** very thin due to lack of food – 25 **gaunt** very thin, bony – 26 **Hausa** language of the Hausa people, the largest ethnic group in Nigeria

The day daddy died, Uncle Tayo put his arms around my shoulders and told me to stop crying. We walked to the *kaboki* store down the street and he bought me a bottle of Fanta and a packet of biscuits. We sat in silence in the dimly lit living room with Mummy, my sisters, Uncle Segun, Aunty Titi, and Aunty Fisayo. Uncle Tayo sat in daddy's chair. I sat beside him, resting my head against his chest. Mummy dabbed tears away from her eyes with her wrapper from time to time. Neighbors trickled in and out of our house. They all had puzzled expressions and different explanations for daddy's mysterious death.

Mrs. Delano, who lived across the street and had a son who was a doctor in London, said that she saw a star fall from the sky the previous night when she went outside to take down clothes she had washed earlier in the day. Mr. Omotosho, who was the headmaster of a small private school on the street before my street, said he had seen a black cat sitting in front of our gate just that morning. Paapa, a white-haired man who had lived the longest on our street, said he saw a dark cloud over our house in a dream he'd had some days before. He said he'd shared the dream with his wife and they'd prayed about it.

That night I dreamt about black cats and dark ominous clouds.

The next morning, Uncle Tayo woke me with a heavy slap. His hand left an imprint on my face. He dragged me from my bed and pushed me to the floor. When I opened my eyes, I saw Uncle Segun, Aunty Titi, and Aunty Fisayo standing behind Uncle Tayo. I heard my mother crying loudly behind my door.

"You and your witch mother are leaving this house today, illegitimate goat," Uncle Tayo said as he kicked me. "We will kill you before you kill us." Aunty Titi and Aunty Fisayo nodded. Uncle

---

2 **kaboki** *Lebensmittelladen* – 21 **ominous** threatening, dangerous-looking –
28 **illegitimate** *here: unehelich*

Segun shouted insults at my mother in Yoruba. He slapped her and she fell to the floor. For the first time, I wished that Uncle Segun's eyes would go blind. He already had poor and rapidly deteriorating vision because of his albinism. I get lost in my thoughts every time I recall that day, particularly Uncle Segun's pale hand slicing across the air before landing on Mummy's cheeks. The memory is like paddling out into the vast lagoon without the backdrop of Makoko to guide you back home where you set out from.

It was only when my mother slammed the door that I realized that she and Iya Tubosun had run out of hurtful words to throw at each other and that the crowd which had gathered had dispersed. Mummy threw herself on the mattress and slept for the rest of the day. She did not let me or my sisters go outside to play, so we were stuck inside with her. The next morning, I tiptoed outside while she was still asleep. An unpleasant smell of feces and trash hung in the air. It had rained heavily throughout the night and outside was dull and heavy, as if a lot more rain was still to come.

I felt myself unfold as soon as I stepped out. It was as if all the air outside inflated my whole body, not just my lungs. Tubosun was sitting on the ten-inch wide plank that was their front porch; his legs spilled over the edge and dangled in the dirty water below, which had risen because of the rains. He was biting his nails and scratching dried flakes of skin from the infection on his scalp. He often sat outside like this whenever his mother had a client inside. His brother and his sisters would come to my house or go to some other friend's house. But Tubosun never joined them. He preferred to sit alone and bite his nails.

---

11 **to disperse** to go away – 15 **feces** [ˈfiːsiːz] (*pl*) *Fäkalien, Kot* – 23 **scalp** skin on top of the head

I asked him if Jide was home. I wanted us to paddle out into the lagoon. Tubosun pretended not to hear me. I raised my voice and asked him again. He looked at me through the corners of his eyes, rolled his eyeballs and hissed loudly. He got up from the edge of the plank that he sat on and walked to the end that was farthest away from me. I watched as his hips swayed from side to side in an intentionally exaggerated fashion.

This was his way of reacting to the fight between our mothers.

I wanted to call him a bastard. The word hung from the tip of my tongue. It was what his mother called him.

When she and Mummy were friends, she would come to our house complaining about things he had done that displeased her. "I no know who give me that bastard. No be same person who give me Jide," she'd say, laughing. The first time I heard her call him a bastard, I'd been startled at the casual ease of it, as if it was normal. That day on the porch I didn't call Tubosun a bastard out of fear that Jide might hear me.

Although Jide was younger, he struck a strange fear in me. There was something about his authoritative demeanor, the stiffness and seriousness of his face, the broadness of his chest that belied his age. He was taller and stronger than both Tubosun and me. He usually decided where we paddled to, what games we played, and how long we spent on an activity. I sometimes imagined him as one of the soldiers in daddy's stories about the Buhari regime, which in its time had authorized soldiers to flog adult men and women for petty things like not forming a line when entering public transportation. Even at eleven, Jide already had a manliness that I and the other boys lacked. He probably thought of himself as the only male and,

---

19 **demeanor** the way sb behaves – 24 **Buhari regime** Major-General Muhammadu Buhari (*1942) was one of the leaders of the military coup in 1983 and served as Nigeria's head of state until 1985. He once again became head of state in the presidential elections of 2015. – 25 **to flog** to whip

perhaps, the de facto first-born in his house. Sometimes I felt that his masculinity was so conspicuous because it stood in stark contrast to his older brother's femininity.

Tubosun was not like the other boys in the neighborhood. He never joined us for our fishing trips. He preferred to play hand and leg games with the girls. Once, when I and the boys came back from fishing, we sat in the boat and watched as Tubosun and some girls played Ten Ten in front of his house. In the middle of the foot-stomping rhythms, one girl's braided extension dropped from her head and Tubosun picked it up and attached it to his own. He ran his hands over the length of hair repeatedly and tucked it behind his ear. The other boys and I laughed.

Jide glanced at us and our laughter vanished instantly.

As Tubosun continued to bite his nails and stare into the distance at nothing in particular, I asked him about Jide one last time.

This time he did not look in my direction. I realized that he was determined to ignore me, so I sighed and went home.

I heard him stutter "p-p-p-pra-pra-pra-prancing beggar" and burst into laughter behind me as I closed the door.

Later that afternoon, Mummy finally got up from the mattress where she had been sleeping since she came inside after her fight with Iya Tubosun the previous day. Her eyes were dim, as if she'd been crying throughout the time she'd slept. A dried, flaky trail of spit adorned the left corner of her mouth. Her short hair was tangled and pointed straight out of her head, as if in rebellion against something she had done or not yet done.

My sisters and I watched her as she picked out a flowery shirt from among her few clothes, which sat in a pile at the edge of the mattress. But just as she was about to slip into it, she remembered

---

2 **conspicuous** obvious, apparent – 23 **flaky** coming off in small, flat, thin pieces

that Iya Tubosun had given her the shirt, so she threw it back into the pile and settled on a sleeveless yellow shirt instead. Mummy knew that we were watching her, so she took extra precautions to avoid making eye contact with our hungry faces. No one had eaten anything since the previous morning. Mummy bent over the kerosene stove and shook it to see if it had any kerosene. It was empty.

But even if it had kerosene, I wasn't sure what she would have cooked. Almost all the money my mother earned went to keeping the rusted corrugated iron sheet roof over our heads. Mummy straightened herself, put her hands on her waist, and shook her head. "Ade, you have to work," she said to me, without making eye contact. "You can see how tight things are. I will ask the Holy Prophet to pray for you so that you can get a job."

The next week, I started working as a gateman at a school in Victoria Island, the business center of Lagos. I got the job through a member of our church, who was also a gateman at the school. It was my first opportunity to leave Makoko. As much as the stench of Makoko and the lagoon had become a part of my identity, they did not have the same hold on me that they had on most residents. Every night I dreamt of the day when I would leave Makoko and never return. In my dreams, I always load a big suitcase into a canoe and then paddle out of the lagoon and all the way to Murtala Mohammed International Airport, where I get on a flight to America and start a new life.

In reality, I would need to board one or two rickety *danfo* buses— the ubiquitous small yellow vehicles, black stripes along their sides, that are a unique feature of the Lagos landscape—to get to the airport.

---

10 **corrugated** *gewellt* – 26 **rickety** fragile, likely to break – 26 **danfo buses** yellow minibuses used as public transport – 27 **ubiquitous** present everywhere

Later, when I was paid my first salary, I folded the few notes into my pocket and took three *danfo* buses from the school to my late father's house in Surulere.

It was my first time there since my mother, my sisters and I were chased out. The bright red gate, which was one of the few things that I remembered about the house, was now painted black. An image of the day when I crashed into the gate and bruised my knee with the new bicycle that was my seventh birthday present from my father floated into my memory. I wrapped my hands around the bars at the top of the black gate and broke into tears, which surprised me.

I had only returned to get closure, to bury a stubborn memory that had refused to die with time. I had not thought about what I would say or how I would react if I ran into Uncle Tayo or my father's other siblings, whom I'd not seen since the day they sent us packing.

As I wept in front of the gate, I did not notice that a grey, 1997 Toyota Corolla had pulled over beside the gate and a man dressed in a business casual outfit had stepped out of the car and was walking towards me.

"Can I help you?" he asked, fidgeting with a big bunch of keys in his left hand.

Words eluded me. I tried to speak. Only salty tears came. The man was patient, but I could see anxiety seeping into his chest. He was ready to fight or to run if he had to. After three attempts, I managed to tell him only about the memory of my bruised knee. He looked more confused than he was before. That was when my words finally came back to me and I told him everything. The man, who looked like he was between fifty-five and sixty-five, kept his

---

17 **to weep** (wept, wept) to cry – 23 **to elude** if sth eludes you, you cannot find or remember it

hands in his pockets while I spoke. His brows were furrowed. He did not interrupt or ask any questions until I'd finished.

I asked him if he had bought the house from Uncle Tayo. But he had never heard the name before. He said that he bought the house from an Igbo man, who had bought the house from a Yoruba man, whom he believed was the original owner of the house.

"When I bought this house," he said, biting on his lower lip, "it was in a bad state. I had to do a lot of work on it."

I pointed at Mrs. Delano's house across the street and asked whether she still lived there. His eyes widened and he smiled at me for the first time. It seemed the question was his first authentication of my story.

Mrs. Delano, who'd said she'd seen a star fall when my father died, had moved to London two years earlier. She wanted to be closer to her son.

I was restless on my way back to Makoko that night. My heart pounded heavily against the walls of my chest. It could barely contain the exhilaration of what had transpired that day. My head felt light and free. My lips ached to tell someone about the man, the bright red gate, which was now black, and Mrs. Delano.

I couldn't tell my mother what I'd done. Any mention of my father made her face fall with the weight of sadness. I decided to stop by Iya Tubosun's house on my way home to tell Jide everything. I could already picture his eyes lighting up at my story about my father's house. I looked forward to providing embellished answers to any questions that he would ask.

---

18 **exhilaration** very happy and excited feeling – 25 **to embellish** to make more interesting or beautiful

No one was sitting outside on the porch when I knocked on Iya Tubosun's door that evening. That should have been a clue to me that something was wrong. Tubosun and his siblings usually ate their dinner outside on the porch. Although I heard voices inside, no one answered the door. I knocked again.

There was no response for a while, but just as I was about to head home, Iya Tubosun shouted, "*Ta ni ye*? Who is that?" She opened the door as soon as she confirmed that it was me.

Once I stepped inside, a ravenous shock descended on me and consumed all the excitement that had been bubbling within. Iya Tubosun's house was dark, except for a dull glow that emanated from the kerosene lamp that hung overhead on a hook attached to the ceiling.

In the dark, Tubosun lay motionless on the floor. His face was swollen beyond recognition. Cuts and bruises covered his entire body. He had been caught kissing another boy at school that afternoon.

An angry mob had formed and beat the two boys. I didn't witness the beating since I no longer went to school. The outcome may have been worse had Jide not gone to the scene just in time. He'd been heroic when he stepped in and fought off the boys who were beating his brother. But he had not escaped unharmed. An old shirt was wrapped around the gash on Jide's head.

He and Tubosun were expelled on the spot. The principal said he didn't want an abomination at his school. While I stood just inside the door, Iya Tubosun sat restlessly on a short stool in a corner, shouting, "Bastard, bastard, bastard," repeatedly in Yoruba. She shifted her chin from one palm to the other every few moments.

---

9 **ravenous** *here*: very great – 11 **to emanate** to come from – 18 **mob** *here*: large group of people – 23 **gash** wound, cut – 25 **abomination** sth that causes great disgust and dislike

I couldn't tell whether the redness in her eyes was from crying, since her eyes were always red. But her voice was cracked and she spoke without the certainty that I had come to know very well.

I knew it would not be wise to bring up my story, so I only sympathized with Iya Tubosun and her family and promised to check on them the next day.

When I went home, I tried to read the first pages of the used novel I bought earlier that day. The sentences on the pages of the book merged into a blurry image of the red gate, and I could hardly focus. I blew out my candle and forced myself to sleep.

In my dream that night, I loaded the familiar suitcase into Mummy's canoe and paddled to the airport. I got on a flight that stopped in London, where I saw a grey-haired Mrs. Delano. I told her that I was on my way to America.

Make notes here on what this section has contributed to
your bigger picture of "Voices of Africa – Nigeria"